ATTENTION, READER: PLEASE NOTE THAT THIS IS NOT A FINISHED BOOK.

An advance readers copy is the first stage of printer's proofs, which has not been corrected by the author, publisher, or printer.

The design, artwork, page length, and format are subject to changes, and typographical errors will be corrected during the course of production.

If you quote from this advance readers copy, please indicate that your review is based on uncorrected text.

Thank you.

SUFFER A WITCH
A MEMOIR

JOY MCCULLOUGH

ISBN: 9780593855904
Trim: 6" x 9"
On Sale: August 2026
336 pages
$30.00 USA / $41.99 CAN
Dutton Books

SUFFER A WITCH

a memoir

JOY McCULLOUGH

DUTTON BOOKS

DUTTON BOOKS
An imprint of Penguin Random House LLC
1745 Broadway, New York, NY 10019
penguinrandomhouse.com

Copyright © 2026 by Joy McCullough

Scripture quotations taken from The Holy Bible, New International Version®, NIV®. Copyright © 1973, 1978, 1984, 2011 by Biblica, Inc. Used with permission of Zondervan. All rights reserved worldwide. www.zondervan.com

Penguin Random House values and supports copyright. Copyright fuels creativity, encourages diverse voices, promotes free speech, and creates a vibrant culture. Thank you for buying an authorized edition of this book and for complying with copyright laws by not reproducing, scanning, or distributing any part of it in any form without permission. You are supporting writers and allowing Penguin Random House to continue to publish books for every reader. Please note that no part of this book may be used or reproduced in any manner for the purpose of training artificial intelligence technologies or systems.

Dutton is a registered trademark of Penguin Random House LLC.

Design by Anna Booth
Text set in Edita Regular

Library of Congress Cataloging-in-Publication Data is available.

Manufactured in the United States of America
[vendor code TK]

ISBN 9780593855904
10 9 8 7 6 5 4 3 2 1 | $PrintCode

The authorized representative in the EU for product safety and compliance is Penguin Random House Ireland, Morrison Chambers, 32 Nassau Street, Dublin D02 YH68, Ireland, https://eu-contact.penguin.ie.

To the angry girl,
to the girl who tells her truth,
to the girl who keeps her truth,

    if you find yourself in these pages,
    I'm so sorry. It wasn't your fault.

        I wrote this for you.

SUFFER
A WITCH

PROLOGUE

At three years old
I stood in the pulpit
of St. Giles' Cat hedral
Edinburgh's mother church of Presbyterianism,
and declared I would be a preacher.

Seven years old,
I stood in the pulpit
of another Presbyterian church
in the San Diego suburbs
and recited my assigned passage
for the Nine Lessons and Carols
        (*In the beginning was the Word*)
even though I'd spiked a fever.

Twelve years old,
I played Jesus in *Godspell*
walking down the aisle
of the same sanctuary
sermonizing to my disciples,
on the edge of adolescence
eager to devour the world.

But at sixteen years old,
I was meant to play Mary Magdalene
at the tomb on Easter morning

        —oh Mary Magdalene,
        apostle turned whore
        by the cowardice of men—

but I panicked
backed out
unable to trust

my body
my voice

too aware
the sanctuary
was anything but.

I am a girl
whose father
is the senior pastor

of a church
that hires a youth pastor
who abuses his eldest daughter
and when she tells her father
        (Our Father)
before she leaves for college
he keeps the youth pastor on staff

and when my sister asks our father
if they should tell me
just a freshman to her senior

our father says no
they shouldn't ruin
my youth group experience.

After high school
after college
after him

I learn about
Artemisia Gentileschi

a seventeenth-century painter
whose father hired a tutor
to teach her perspective
and the tutor raped her

and it wasn't the father's fault
        exactly
except that
he knew the tutor's reputation
she shouldn't have been left alone
he shouldn't have been given access

and a girl
who has had perspective forced upon her
can never unlearn the lesson.

Artemisia will change my life.

I first read Artemisia's name
as an intriguing reference
in a novel I could swear was
The Robber Bride by Margaret Atwood
but I will scour that book years later
and then all of Atwood's books
and find no mention of her

but I take my curiosity
to the nascent internet
and when I find only crumbs
that intrigue me more.

I end up
in the art history aisle
of my local library

enraptured
not so much by the art
in the pages

      which is masterful

but by the transcript
in the back of the book
translated from the Italian
for a trial in which a man
is accused of damaging
another man's property
by raping her.

I must write Artemisia's story
and I am a playwright

      —I'll never write a book,
      of that I'm certain—

so I begin writing a play

but facing Artemisia's story
      and its similarities to mine
is frightening
so I keep my distance

by writing a play
that is mostly about
an art history professor
who specializes in Artemisia Gentileschi
and as she lectures her students
the scenes unfold from her most famous works

but then the professor's brother
shows up in town, unexpected,
and dredges up old memories
and the art history professor
must face her own trauma.

That version of the play
didn't work

but I wasn't wrong
about how the trauma survivor
must face their deepest pain
over and over
until they think they've faced all there is to face
and then something unexpected
rears up into monstrous form
and the survivor
must claw and scrape
for their survival again

that in fact survival
is never in the past tense

that healing isn't linear
and even the people
who are supposed to love
a survivor most
might bring with that love
horrors
that could eclipse
the original trauma.

I am determined
to make Artemisia's story work.
I figure out
that I need to strip away
the entire layer
of the professor's story

        a scalpel peeling away
        long-dried layers of paint.

                I'd thought
                I was making it more relatable
                but really
                I was protecting myself
                by avoiding
                the raw, unfiltered story.

I focus the play on Artemisia
as she works on her paintings
of the biblical Judith and Susanna
but she's only painting them,
instead of engaging with their truth.

It still doesn't work.
But it's getting closer.

Finally I realize
I need to face Artemisia's story
and she needs to face Judith's and Susanna's stories
and they need to face the stories told from the beginning of time from the
    first woman who was blamed
when she did nothing but try to survive.

I could scrape off
every bit of paint
and I'd be left
with a blank canvas.

Instead
I need to burn
the whole studio down
this studio built for men's expression
their version of events

and only then
can we all move forward.

We will show each other
what a woman can do.

PART I

Exodus 22:18
Thou
shalt not suffer

      a witch
      to live.

Eve.
First, but not.
Creation's revision.
Innocent temptress.

Even as a child
on a hard wooden pew
I understand
born of a rib
is demeaning

but better than
born of dirt.

It seems unfair
to be stuck with some guy
you didn't choose,
who didn't choose you

but then again
they were made
for each other,
intentional,
and that's something.

God doesn't make
mistakes.

Those trees in the garden,
the ones God said
not to touch
with their plump fruits
weighing down the branches
in my children's Bible

tempting me
to reach grubby fingers
into that pristine garden
and steal a bite,

Adam never
gives them
a second glance.

      Not the way
      they tell us
      the story, anyway.

Obedience, I understand
as a pastor's daughter.
But I also have to think,
memorize my scripture,
be the first to shoot my hand
into the air with answers.

Adam does what he's told
and drops to sleep
the moment he curls his body
around Eve's at night.

But Eve lies awake, head buzzing.

If I'd appeared fully formed
in this garden of delights
I'd have had endless questions too.

What does this taste like,
smell like, feel like?
Why do tiny flying creatures
dive into fragrant blooms?
Why are most things for our pleasure
but those trees forbidden?

Why is there a talking snake?

Adam is there too.

Scholars bend over backward
flexible as the snake itself
to imagine a scene where only Eve
succumbs to the serpent's temptation
to eat the forbidden fruit

and only when she offers it
does simple Adam eat.
Almost as a favor to her,
doesn't want to hurt her feelings.

        I should have noticed
        how the woman was blamed
        while the man stood by,
        wide-eyed, somehow innocent
        meanwhile wielding all the power.

        If I had looked beyond the primary colors
        of the cartoon snake and rosy red apple,
        noticed these absurd twists in the story,
        would things have turned out differently?

        When the serpent came for me,
        would I have seen him for what he was?
        When the man was weak in his power,
        would I have fled the garden
        as fast as bare feet could carry me
        over rocky, punishing ground?

        But that's assuming
        there was a way
        out of the garden
        for either of us.

Here's what I do notice
as a child formed by a church
with a father who preaches
                            predestination:

God made the tree with irresistible fruit
and the serpent to tempt her

then watched as events unfolded
exactly as he planned

and punished her for it.

Before I formed you
in the womb I knew you
and before you were born
I set you apart.

                    Before God formed me
                    in my mother's womb
                    she worked to put my father
                    through seminary

In him we were also chosen
having been predestined
according to the plan of him

                    and after long days teaching
                    junior high, she'd take my father's
                    handwritten essays and type them

who works out everything
in conformity with the
the purpose of his will.

                    and one late night while my father slept
                    she found herself transcribing
                    his fervent argument for predestination

The Lord works out everything
to its proper end: even the wicked
for a day of disaster.

                    but she resisted:

                          if everything was already decided
                          what was the point in any of this?

*For those God foreknew,
he also predestined
to be conformed
to the image of his Son.*

                                        but it wasn't her place to argue
                                        to think for herself
                                        and so instead she typed and cried
                                        and ate an entire bag of chocolate chips.

*In all things
God works for the good
of those who love him.*

Eve's punishment:
cast out of the garden

but is it a punishment
to escape a trap
designed for her fall?

The real punishment comes
when God curses her

curses all who bear children
with painful labor and submission to men.

> (That last part, that's the real kicker,
> slipped in there like we might not notice.)

Not only childbirth but
every monthly discomfort
comes back to Eve, I'm taught.

I never blamed her, though.
Eve, who bled for the first time
without a mother, a sister, a friend
to guide the way,
Eve who was seized
with labor pains and pushed out
brand-new, writhing, helpless humans
with no idea what was happening,
believing it to be her end.

Eve, who sought knowledge.

Dear Eufame,

Did you know, as your belly grew round, how your babes would finally emerge? How your muscles would contract so fiercely you'd have confessed to any evildoing in order to make the torture stop?

You couldn't have been completely ignorant. Women talk. You didn't have apps to track your ovulation, message boards comparing symptoms. But even as a noblewoman, you'd have attended births. At the very least, you'd have listened from the next room as sisters, cousins, aunts brought forth life, while you sipped wine, trying to maintain your decorum, as though that agony wouldn't come for you one day too.

When it did, the pain ripped through you, the worst you'd ever known. How do women do this again and again? Shouldn't once be enough to learn the lesson and take every measure possible to avoid another round of this torture?

We forget, they say, because our babies are so angelic. But we don't forget any more than a soldier forgets the most gruesome battle. We're simply that strong.

You would have been, too, if you'd lived to birth another child.

To call the whole thing poor design would be blasphemy, and while I may have strayed, you were a good Protestant. Of course new life comes at a cost. Of course all women are cursed with labor pains, going back to that witch Eve.

That's what the men said, anyway, and who could question them? They were God's voice on earth, after all.

You simply had to dig deep, summon strength you never knew you had. Easy as that. But it stretched on through the night and into the day. Blinding pain, you'd rather have died. (Careful what you wish for.)

The plans you made for how it would go were as naive as a woman seeking power. The doctors, the nurses, the midwives, each with their own agendas, their assumptions, their drugs to force the baby out on their schedules—

But wait, I'm sorry. We are descended through Eve, succulent fruits cascading branch to branch through the tree of knowledge, but we are not the same, you and I.

For one thing, Eufame, the midwife claimed two babies grew inside you. Oh, how I feel for you. One foreign invader at a time—however dearly wanted—was torture enough for me. Perhaps you'd seen this before; twins do run in families. You wouldn't have understood the science, but you'd have known whether the mothers survived the birth. You might have known they often didn't, in your day, when two babies jostled for who would emerge first. So eager to enter the world, but the cost could be all your lives.

The pains eased only for moments—a sip of ale, a rag to the brow, and then you were in it again. (They told me contractions would come in waves, there would be time in between to recover. They were wrong. We are not the same, but I feel sure we are, in this.) In one of those moments of respite your brain cleared enough for this thought: the God who cursed Eve's womb and all those who came after her was the vengeful Old Testament God. The one who flooded the world. The one who asked Abraham to murder his own son. Who piled trauma after trauma upon his most faithful servant, Job, just to prove he could.

But you were a Protestant. You knew that the vengeful God's son brought compassion, bore the sins of the world. Unlike those Catholics with their penance and self-flagellations, with their statues of Jesus forever suffering, Protestants revere the empty cross.

He is risen.

He is love and grace and mercy. He suffered for you, so why should you suffer like this?

The pains came again, a cresting wave that never fell, crucifixion without resurrection, you would die and your babies too.

But you didn't—not yet. The next time you could spare the energy to form words, you asked the midwife if there wasn't something she could do to ease your pain?

Anyone in your place would have done the same. In brutal agony, anyone would grasp for relief. A witch under questioning. A soldier on the battlefield. Even Jesus on the cross cried out to his God, his Father, asking why he had been forsaken.

The midwife had heard this request before, of course she had. All the births she'd attended, her own births. It's the rare mother who doesn't plead for help. It still is.

But 1591, oh it's so early. How you'd marvel at something as simple as aspirin. The epidural I scorned is beyond the scope of your imagination. You would have taken whatever the midwife had to give. And you did.

Her remedy included:

- a lock of hair from a virgin half your age
- twelve ants, dried in an oven warm from baking bread
- a quarter pint of milk from a red cow
- and the finger, toe, and knee joints of disinterred corpses

It's easy now to scoff at this ludicrous remedy. But it's less amusing with the knowledge of how you'll pay for it.

Somehow you survived the labor—perhaps giving the midwife confidence in her remedy of virgin hair and corpse joints—and you convalesced. The agonizing ordeal had taken a disastrous toll on your body. You could still have died. Each time you stood you were sure your insides would fall out. The chamber pot brought you back to the worst moments of labor.

It seemed you'd never stop bleeding.

The midwife called it normal.

The worst was when the babies suckled. Medicine didn't yet understand that nipple stimulation causes uterine contractions, but as each baby was nourished and comforted, you were back in agony, oh God, it was happening again.

When someone knocked on the door, you hoped for the midwife with some bit of comfort or relief more effective than virgin hair, and not a busybody neighbor who'd expect you to receive guests and delight in the miracle (the agony) of birth.

You could never have imagined—even the midwife, after all the births she'd seen couldn't have imagined—that it would be the king's men at your door, there to yank you from your bed, trailing blood, arresting you for violating God's commandment:

> Unto the woman he said,
> "I will greatly multiply thy sorrow and thy conception;
> in sorrow thou shalt bring forth children;
> and thy desire shall be to thy husband,
> and he shall rule over thee."

Simply by requesting relief from the pains of childbirth, you had violated the law of God and by extension, the law of the king, who personally ordered your execution.

You couldn't make sense of it. How could the monarch, with an entire kingdom to run, possibly trouble himself with something so small? Why should he care? Had he never felt pride or jealousy or lust? Had he never broken a commandment? Of course he had, and more.

They lashed your hands behind you, around the stake. A splinter wedged itself in your wrist and you almost laughed at the pain. A splinter, when you could already choke on the smoke from the torches?

Neither pain had anything on childbirth.

Sometimes, in the years to come, they'll hang the women they call witches before they burn them. More merciful, they'll tell themselves. Maybe more merciful for the onlookers, who don't have to hear the agonized wails of the women. If the onlookers close their eyes and ignore the stench of burning flesh, it almost sounds like someone in labor.

The last face you saw before the flames devoured you was not your husband's, or your children's, but that of the midwife who tried to walk with you through that rite of womanhood.

She'll burn too. But not yet.

So many women will burn, and hang, and suffer wild accusations. They won't be trusted to know their own bodies, their minds, their power. So many women will fight back, seek knowledge, defend their sisters.

Refuse to let them chop down the tree of knowledge to burn us. From Eve to you, from you to me, our stories are the fruit on that cursed tree, and they're bursting with sharp, sweet wisdom.

I'm ravenous for all of it. Let me at that fruit.

Eufame MacAlyane
(c 1558–1591, Scotland)
Eufame was a Scottish noblewoman who requested pain relief from the midwife while in labor with twins. King James VI felt this violated God's commandment that women suffer in childbirth and had her burnt alive.

I'm not ready
for labor.
No one ever is
        at least not for their first
but my body excels
at resisting the inevitable.

The women
in my family
hold out weeks beyond
medicine's timetables.
The doctors, midwives call us
                past due
but we define our own normal.

They don't listen,
inject drugs to force
contractions around my baby
who isn't ready either.
She refuses to leave.

I've created her a refuge
where no one else can
tell her a story about
her body. So she endures
her safe home's revolt

ignores the ones
who believe they know better.

I'm not afraid
of the needle.
I've had one in my spine before.
But I'm terrified to lose control
of my baby's safe haven

don't want something shoved
inside me without my consent.
They do it anyway.

That's happened before too.

My body knows
it's wrong.
My heart breaks
in protest,
embargoes blood.
Baby's heart
does the same,
our hearts
beating in sync

until they don't.

race
to the operating room
no chance to consent

doctors, nurses
husband a stranger in scrubs

I vomit lying down
body still fighting
even though
there's no turning back

it will save my life and my baby's
but the body doesn't operate on logic
my body clings to memory
hands forced inside
against my wishes

something taken from me
before my body is ready

before I'm ready

I hurry
because even at seven years old
I know we can't be late.

My father stands in the pulpit
every Sunday morning
but tonight
at this special holiday service
I'm special too.

The first scripture
in the Nine Lessons and Carols
always goes to a young reader

though not usually
as young as I am but

I am the pastor's
daughter, the actress,
so precocious

I can handle
the pressure,
the complicated language:

> *In the beginning was the Word*
> *and the Word was with God*
> *and the Word was God.*

My stomach turns
as we make the short drive
from home to church
for the Nine Lessons and Carols,
where instead of sitting up on the chancel
in his cool gray robes like usual
my pastor-father will sit with his family
in the pew, in a crisp, dark suit.

My head aches
as we make our way
through the narthex—
we're celebrities, greeting our people.
Everyone wants to talk to the pastor
and we're an extension of him.

My cheeks burn
as we take our seats.
It's excitement, not nerves.
I triumphed as Roo
in *Winnie-the-Pooh*.
A simple scripture
for an audience that loves me?
Nothing easier.

But as the sanctuary fills,
my head pounds, limbs go weak.
I slump against the hard pew.
My father nudges me to sit up.

I don't feel well.

He doesn't react.
I appeal to my mother.

I really don't feel well.

She presses a cool hand
to my forehead,
admits I'm warm.
My father frowns.

    You'll be fine.

The choir files in.
Soon it will be my turn.

Daddy, I really think I'm sick.

Sick of the perfect family
that's never late
no hair out of place
shined shoes and smiling faces
each with our own role:

    Mother dieting herself out of existence
    older sister quiet and demure, always knows her scripture
    and I the performer, who must perform.

    Joy, my father says. *Buck up.*

In the Beginning
was the Word
and the Word was God
and the Word was with God

and a little girl
plays her part to perfection
through a spiking fever,
congregation swimming before her,
Father approving in the front row

and she learns
that even if she speaks her truth
there are more important things.

Dear Dorothy,

The youngest person jailed for witchcraft in Salem deserves to have her name remembered correctly. You didn't deserve to be written out of your story by a careless magistrate who couldn't see the difference between one accursed girl and the next and scribbled your name on the arrest warrant as Dorcas.

Somehow that misnomer stuck, but I haven't forgotten your name was Dorothy. How could I ever forget a single thing about you from the moment I learned a four-year-old was not only accused, but tortured and imprisoned for nearly a year because of some fanciful stories she told?

When she was four, my daughter told stories of magical lands and elves and fairies and talking trees. I wouldn't have batted an eye if she told a story like yours of a snake that spoke to her.

But when you told that story, you were no longer seen as a child whose imagination painted pictures so vivid the rest of us couldn't perceive them. No, that story, that snake emerged after weeks of interrogation. The same questions over and over again. Probably they brought up serpents. The truth wasn't enough to make them stop, so you were clever. You used what they gave you and came up with something new to tell them.

Only that didn't make it stop. That led to examinations of your tiny body—stripping you down and searching for marks of the devil like they claimed they'd found on your mother.

How she howled when they tore you from her.

There's no account of it, of your mother's love, because it didn't matter to the men who wrote the story. But it matters to me. She would have protected you, if she could. I hope you knew that.

When they threw you in a prison cell with no sunlight, no one to look after you, nothing but a square of cloth to busy your hands, were you still young enough to imagine this might be some kind of twisted game? Or had they already broken you?

How long did you scream for help before you realized no one was coming?

In the years since my own dark cell, people assume I should be fine. So much time has passed. *(You can't play the abuse card forever.)* But you know. Even after your release, it wasn't over. You did not hang like your mother, but you broke all the same. The rest of your life you lived in the darkness.

I will shine light on your story, Dorothy.

Dorothy Good
(c 1688–c 1717, Salem, MA)
Dorothy was imprisoned for almost a year as a four- to five-year-old. Her mother, Sarah, was executed and her baby sister died in prison. Dorothy was released when her father could put together the bail funds, but she never mentally recovered.

When the baby
who was ripped from my body
before she was ready
before I was ready
is squinting in the daylight
streaming through
my hospital window

she does not leave my side
unless she is with her papa
and when she cries
she is always held
even when she cries
all night for years

and I worry that my trauma
is etched into her bones
and even though she's safe
I will fight any monster to be sure
but she screams because she knows
the world outside would imprison
a helpless girl for telling a story.

A Presbyterian church
is designed in the shape
of a cross as seen from above.
The front where the pastor speaks
the choir sings
the children play Mary and Joseph
is the top of the cross
where Jesus's head might have rested
at least until his crown of thorns
pierced his scalp.

To the sides
there are two wings called transepts
with seating for those who would sit

where Jesus's arms
were spread wide
dripping blood

The main seating area
is the rest of the cross
where his body hung
his side was pierced

and it didn't strike me
until adulthood

how strange it is
to build
an entire religion's
iconography
its very stones
and foundation
around the shape
of the torture device
used to execute
their savior.

It's rather like
building a palace
in the shape
of a guillotine

a barn
in the shape
of a butcher's knife

or a school
in the shape of a gun.

My childhood church
is modern
for the time
clean lines
no stained glass
or ornate woodwork.

Three Sunday morning services
fill a space
that seats six hundred.

The earliest service at 8 a.m.
has guitars and a band
leading contemporary worship songs

the next two services
            9:30 and 11:00
are more traditional
with hymns
and a choir of eighty singers,
known in the area
as one of the best.

It's not a megachurch
but it's not small either
and between services
the churchgoers mingle
in the always sunny courtyard,
lucky to live in the San Diego suburbs
lucky to have found
                such a perfect church.

My father presides
over all three services
and sits up front
in his gray-and-black robes.

Sunday school is at 9:30
so I attend a service
before or after.

        I must have sat
        with my mother and sister
        at least until my sister
        was in high school
        and wanted to sit
        with her friends

        but I have
        no memory of that.

        I do remember
        where I liked to sit
        and continued to sit
        in high school
        when I went alone

                my sister off to college
                and my mother
                busy with other responsibilities
                in the unpaid, high-labor role
                of pastor's wife

        on the left-hand side
        center aisle
        of the main sanctuary area
        four rows back.

FRESHMAN YEAR

I've just moved up
from junior high youth group
····all juvenile games I hate
to the high school group
with a soda fountain in the meeting room
and my sister with her friends
singing They Might Be Giants

········the esoteric lyrics
········another layer
········of their sophistication as seniors

and Tom, the youth pastor
a beloved family friend
since I was reciting scripture
for the Nine Lessons and Carols

but halfway through
my freshman year
Tom is moving up, too,
on to a different job in another state.

When Tom became the youth pastor
I was still a child
playing paper dolls
at his house
with his daughter.

Too young to understand
why Tom requested
that a window be cut
into the door of his office

for he realized
that a grown man
who counsels young people
must put their safety first.

> *Opacity is fear,*
> my daughter tells me,
> talking about something else
>   entirely,
> quoting playwright Sarah Ruhl
> on the same day
> Tom's wife tells me
> about the window
> in the door.

As the window was being cut
my father, Tom's boss,
came down the hallway.

> *What's this?*

Tom explained
to my father

why a grown man
who counsels people
who put their trust in him
should be worthy of that trust.

My father huffed,
rolled his eyes
in exasperation
and walked away.

We're introduced
to the new youth pastor
in the narthex
on his first Sunday.

> (*Narthex*: one of those words
> so familiar to pastors' kids
> while people outside the church
> squint and wonder
> what language we're speaking
> but it's only the iceberg's tip
> of this inscrutable world.)

Someone

                                      I don't remember who

pulls my sister and me over
after a service
to where he stands

                                      I do remember the exact spot
                                      which direction he was facing
                                      which direction I was facing

with his wife.

> *Girls, come meet*
> *the new youth pastor, M.*

When I began
writing this
I called him M
because thirty years later
I still panic at the sight or sound
of his (very common, everywhere I turn) name

except even the initial
started to cause
a creeping anxiety
which warred with fury

> he cannot take
> a goddamned *letter* from me

and I didn't want
to ruin another name

but if I was going to tell this story
I had to call him something

so I decided to try out
Brett
since that name
had already been ruined
by the news cycles
where we learned
that the world may fully believe
a credible woman's story

> they simply won't care
> to do anything about it.

Or I could call him
Harvey
or Neil
or Matt
or Bill
or Louie
or Roman
or Jeffrey
or Andrew
or Kevin
or Danny
or Bryan
or Larry
or Roger
or Charlie
or Gérard
or Lars
or Jeremy
or Russell
or Mario
or Dustin
or Morgan
or Paul
or James
or Woody
or Casey
or Luc
or Leslie
or Johnny
or Ryan
or Joss
or Frank
or Fred
or Ben
or Bob
or Oliver
or Richard
or Steven

As it turns out
there is no shortage
of names defiled
by the men who bear them.

Brett's wife
is barely older
than my sister.
He's nearly thirty.

                    I learned later
                    that he was a volunteer
                    in his wife's high school youth group
                    and her father was the pastor.

He's chubby, balding,
with warm, brown eyes.
They've come from across the country,
and his young wife speaks
with a Southern drawl, disarming.

                    How many pastors' daughters
                    do you have to pluck from a youth group
                    to make a pattern?
                    Did he know
                    from the moment
                    my sister and I were introduced
                    which one he would target
                                    first?

His pickup
pulls into our driveway

                                        navy blue pickups
                                        send my heart skittering
                                        even now

and I watch from the living room window
as my sister
        so independent, about to graduate
runs out and climbs into the cab
and they drive away together.

I don't know where they're going
but I'm sick with jealousy
that this man sees her
and values her
and listens.

When Brett takes over
he must make do
with Tom's old office

while things are arranged
to move the youth group room
and Brett's office
into a separate portable

and so
Brett tapes
a piece of construction paper
over the window
Tom had cut out
to block the view
to any passerby
of what happens
in that room.

No one objects.

I sprawl
on the floor on my stomach,
legs kicking up behind me,
Bible spread open before me.

A group of girls
hangs out after Bible study
in Brett's living room
singing "Go West Young Man."

Christian pop evoking Manifest Destiny—
take what you want in the name of God.

I giggle with friends,
a freshman trying
to act older than I feel
but not old enough to realize
an adult man might
be noticing my body
in that very moment.

                    He told me later
                    that moment is when
                    I caught his eye

                    my fourteen-year-old ass
                    in leggings during Bible study,
                    a claim for him to stake
                    and blame for inviting his gaze.

Another day
another Bible study
in Brett's living room.

                From the very beginning
                Brett blurred the boundaries
                between church and his private life.
                My father was the senior pastor
                but there were never
                Bible studies in our living room.

During prayer requests,
we say *unspoken*
when we want sympathy
but don't want to give specifics.
An early '90s vague-tweet.

If you really want attention
you ask Brett
if you can speak with him privately.
In his tiny apartment, that means
in his bedroom.

No one finds this strange.
But then, who would?
There are no other adults.

I'm struggling
with my body image, I tell him.

I'm a brunette, growing into curves
rounder than my naturally thin sister
and most of my beach-blond friends

                                (barely
                                there
                                curves,
                                now I see
                                a tiny girl
                                in photos)

and fashion magazines
are telling me I look wrong
while also giving me the language
of self-esteem and body image.

It's all true
but mostly

I want
undivided attention

from a man
who'll look at me

and hear me.
He does.

He's glad I shared that.
I can trust him.

Dear Abigail,

Burnt into my brain, synonymous with your name, is a story not from your telling but from Arthur Miller's pen. His Abigail is wanton and worldly, a femme fatale who rhapsodizes about her lover clutching her back and sweating like a stallion. *The Crucible*'s Abigail accuses Elizabeth Proctor of witchcraft so her lover (her employer) would be free to marry her.

It's a love story, really.

But you were eleven and John Proctor sixty at the time of the Salem witch trials. And besides that, no records show you'd ever met either of the Proctors before accusations began flying.

Perhaps the dramatist bent things to his will for a more compelling story. I do it myself on this very page as I choose your death date: seventeen years after your birth. We don't really know when you died. You might have lived to be eighty-one, like Giles Corey when he was crushed to death by the weight of your accusations (and by the actual stones piled upon his living body because of his alleged crimes).

The difference is, I know what's true and what's fabrication.

Arthur Miller believed the story he wrote, justified it—that you were Eve in the garden, tempting, seducing, destroying the world. And even if that were somehow true—you weren't eleven, but seventeen; you weren't a sheltered Puritan but a wanton femme fatale; you weren't a complete stranger to John Proctor—that all supposes a teenage girl has some power over a man in authority.

I wanted to be you so badly. Not you, the real girl of flesh and bone caught up in the Salem maelstrom, not really. But to play the version of you depicted in *The Crucible*: to tell your story upon a stage, without any understanding of how twisted and misogynist the playwright's version of you was, how yet another powerful man was forcing a young girl to fulfill his depraved desires.

I understand now, Abigail. The truth of your story matters.

Abigail Williams
(1680–1697, Salem, MA)
Abigail was one of the main accusers in Salem, immortalized in *The Crucible* as a seductive teen, but she was only eleven during the Salem witch trials.

SOPHOMORE YEAR

My sister trades the beach
for college in the Windy City
and I'm the only pastor's daughter
     left.

My group of rising sophomores
is *special*
according to Brett.

     As I see it now:
     he wanted to push out
     the older kids,
     the ones who'd had a chance
     to know a youth pastor
     with appropriate boundaries.

Full of strong personalities and leaders,
we quickly fill the ranks of SALT,
the Service and Leadership Team.

SALT means
two-hour meetings every Sunday
between morning services and evening youth group,
helping to run events, leading Bible studies.

Brett claims,
     Adult volunteers
     are basically impossible to recruit,
but he doesn't need them. He has us.

Brett moves the youth group
out of the main administration building
where I've been
watched over
by church staff
since preschool

and into a large portable,
a separate building
so much better

for kids to come and go
without anyone else
realizing who is coming
who is going
who is slipping into Brett's office
while he closes
the windowless door.

During SALT meetings
we sit in a circle
on the floor
of the portable.

Brett always sits beside me.
It's unspoken
but everyone knows—

>always leave
>one space open
>next to Joy
>for Brett.

Our knees bump, shoulders touch.
Long hand-held prayers enclose
my small hand in his overwhelming grip.

We're supposed to call
our prayer partners daily.
Mine is a boy named Dave,
dating my friend April.
He's funny and kind;
decades later, he'll help
my aging mother move.

> *You should be*
> *prayer partners with me.*

Brett is rethinking prayer partners
on one of our endless phone calls.
I talk to him more than Dave
or any of my other friends.

He criticizes Dave, who isn't
academically inclined.
He criticizes April for being silly,
Krista for being uncommitted to God
since she's dancing elite ballet.

He makes fun of my sister for choosing
a conservative Christian college.
He complains relentlessly about my dad, his boss,
and how he just doesn't understand
what Brett needs to do to reach the youth.

But he never criticizes me.

Dear Elizabeth,

A reverend's daughter in Puritan New England and one in 1990s Southern California may not seem very similar at first glance, but the moment I see that descriptor in your story—"reverend's daughter"—I feel a kinship.

The eyes on you, the expectations.

In my day, we're known as PKs—pastors' kids—a role so defined as to have stereotypes. We're either perfectly angelic role models who know every scripture and never have a single stain upon our reputations, or we're wild and unruly rebels.

Which one were you?

My guess is that you were, like me—like every offspring of every clergy member—your own person, sometimes devout and sometimes rebellious, and more often falling somewhere in between.

My guess is that when your friends gathered around the Venus glass to scry their futures, you knew you shouldn't do it, just like I melted into the background at sleepovers during light as a feather, stiff as a board, because it would somehow be against Jesus to play a silly game.

But I also suspect the idea was too tempting, that you might divine your fortune, your future husband. For if we're honest, there'd be no other fortune in your future except the man you'd spend your life with.

Like each of the girls before you, you cracked an egg and dropped the white in a glass of water. Then you searched for meaning in the amorphous shape drifting through the liquid.

If you'd been alone, you could have pretended you didn't immediately see a coffin. It was a . . . pulpit. A jewelry box. A strangely shaped book. A Bible!

But your friends were there, crowded around the glass to see your future too, as Death stared you in the face.

They tried to make the best of it. You'd be a widow, one suggested. Barely married before your husband was lowered into the earth (tragic, but tragedy still seemed romantic then. Besides, you'd be young and able to marry again).

You knew better. This was the natural result of meddling in forbidden things and you were doomed. Unless you could show all of Salem how you resisted the devil.

The thing is, you're more likely to find the devil in the robed men to whom you tell your fantastical story than in a glass of water.

You learned that the hard way, Elizabeth. So did I.

Elizabeth Parris
(1682–1760, Salem, MA)
Elizabeth was one of the main accusers in Salem, and the daughter of the reverend. Early on, her parents sent her away from Salem to escape the hysteria.

Our first SALT retreat
is at Brett's apartment.

> *What does* retreat *mean?*
> my editor asks.
> *Aren't you always*
> *at his apartment?*
>
> Each question
> a realization
> of how bizarre
> this world was,
> how twisted of the adults
> to present it
> as safe and good.

We'll spend the evening
and whole next day
on team building, bonding
and planning youth group events
with a slumber party in between.

No need for other chaperones
since Brett's wife will be there.
Enclosed in her bedroom.

Everyone tumbles together
in sleeping bags on the floor
but I've been granted the couch.
Brett sits on the edge
as everyone falls asleep

but even after
everyone else's breaths have slowed
                                  he stays.

I've never slept well
and passed my nights
as a small child
wandering the halls
while my father
got his doctorate of theology
at the University of Edinburgh
and we rented a drafty flat
in an actual Scottish castle.

Rather than lie awake
in a dark room

>which I shared
>with my older sister
>while she slept soundly
>like a good girl

I would rise
tiny gothic maiden
in footie pajamas
and pace the halls

for if I disturbed my parents
I would only be taken back
to that lonely bed.

Eventually
overtaken by drowsiness
I would crumple where I stood
and my parents would find me
in the morning
asleep on the cold stone floors
of the empty castle hallway.

I'm not alone
at the SALT retreat.

Brett's presence
seated on the end of the couch
where I lie
is comforting

unfamiliar shadows
not so sinister
with a father figure
at the ready

but my father
never spent an entire night
next to me, hand drifting
from my foot
up my leg
to rest
on my hip.

By the next retreat
three more months have passed.
Daily phone calls, rides home,
and through every meeting,
seated at his right hand.

(From there she will come to judge.)

No one is good enough
to be my friend or boyfriend,
sister or parent, but Brett
will always understand me.

We're at Carter's house this time.
Brett's wife isn't there.
Carter's parents chaperone (from upstairs).

I'm on the floor in a sleeping bag.
Again, I never sleep.
Again, Brett at my side
awake until everyone else
has drifted off.

You're so beautiful. Why don't you get that?

He can't see my rising blush
in the hazy darkness.

Tell me what you feel most insecure about.

He only wants to help me.
I know I started this
by going alone
into a room with him

and confessing
my struggles with body image.

That's where this began,
        (It had to be
        because how else
        would I be
        in this position?)
me as temptress, playing that role
I thought I wanted
so badly, Arthur Miller's Abigail,
without ever putting it on my résumé.

        I want to touch
        whatever makes you insecure
        so you know how beautiful it is.

                Did no one hear,
                the room full of my friends?
                Did anyone lie awake with eyes closed,
                listening as this unfolded?
                Did anyone else hear me say

My stomach?

But they wouldn't hear
when Brett slips his hand
inside my sleeping bag
and underneath my T-shirt
to caress my stomach.

The hand drifts
a slippery slope
like Brett preaches about
not down—not yet—
but up and up
to my breasts,
my body frozen.

The hand drifts down
ghosts across my stomach
to the edge of my underwear
and just inside.

       You're so beautiful.

The next day
I've left
                my body.

Brett drives me home.
Not my home
                not my body
but his
        (his wife at work)
and as soon as we're inside
he presses me against his door,
his mouth on mine.

I don't move
            not my body.
I've never been kissed.

        Kiss me back, he orders.

I don't know
what that means.

Soon I'm laid out
on his couch, jean shorts unbuttoned
white T-shirt off, his hands everywhere.

After, he cries.

        I just love you so much.

Dear Salem Girls,

You're the villains in the story, lying teenage girls, clamoring for attention. Except you weren't teenagers; not all of you. Elizabeth and Abigail and Ann, you were nine and eleven and twelve. Children by anyone's standards. If you're older, you see, we're allowed to despise and revile you. I'm not sure where the line is when we shift from compassion for children to laying an atrocity at the feet of teenagers, but it's there.

I've spent way too much time trying to find that line. How old is old enough to bear the weight? I don't know. But it's certainly not nine. Or eleven. Or twelve.

You were children, convinced your fantasies were true. You embellished your accounts to match the scrutiny they received. You were caught up in the feeling of having power, being heard, for once.

And when it was all over—twenty innocents executed, more dead in prison and by suicide, from fear or grief, an entire town devastated and made synonymous with the word *witch*—you would be blamed.

A handful of girls.

It's almost like you really did have power. Enough to overthrow whole systems constructed around you, constricting you. *Puritanical*, a word that means repression as surely as *Salem* means witches.

It's almost like you orchestrated the entire thing, like you didn't need men to file court documents, pass judgments, didn't need the whole of a town to rise up and back your claims out of petty grievances, didn't need a church to seize on the chance to drive people back into the pews from which they'd strayed.

I wish I could tell you that you were powerful. I know what it cost you—what it cost me—to survive. But I won't lie. You never had power.

Brett requires
his followers near him
at all times

which means
they sit with him
in the balcony
during church services

which I try
a few times
but don't like

so even though
I'll pay a price
I insist on sitting
where I want to
where I feel most comfortable
where I can focus
on the service
on the worship

without feeling
eyes on me
expectations
demands for my attention.

I am there to worship

        but not him.

The portable contains
an office for Brett
and an office for Joe

        the junior high youth pastor
        who must trek across campus
        to reach the room
        where his group meets
        so he's rarely in his office

and in between their offices
a storage space

so from Brett's office
you have to go through a door
into the storage space
and from the storage space
you have to go through another door
into Joe's office

which means that if you're in Brett's office
and Joe opens the door into the storage space
you will hear him, you will have warning
before he opens the door into Brett's office.

The three steps between the doors
is plenty of time
to spring apart
and straighten clothes.

I turn sixteen
midway through sophomore year
but I don't get my driver's license.

        My own kids
        and their friends
        are in no rush to drive.
        The always-connected world
        of internet and social media
        means it's easy to be with your friends
        no matter where you're located

        but in the '90s
        most teens got their licenses
        the first moment they could
        because a license meant freedom,
        the ability to get away from parents
        the ability to get to your friends.

I know
that as soon as
I get my license
I will have less freedom than ever.

The Edge
is the name
of the Sunday evening youth meeting

and to be fair
it was called that
even before Brett came

                                    but it's so wild now
                                    to think about
                                    how I was constantly
                                    on edge
                                    on the edge
                                    how blurry
                                    all the edges were.

It starts at 7:17.
Why? Who can say?
It seems edgy?
It's the '90s?
We would never be
so boring and predictable
as to start at 7:00 or 7:30.

Kids begin arriving
at 7:00, more every Sunday
to Brett's giddy delight.
He focuses relentlessly
on numbers.

Numbers mean
we're reaching more kids for God
except mostly they mean
that Brett has more and more followers
who will hang on his every word

spilling out of the portable
too many to be contained
happy in the balmy evening
for it's always balmy
it never changes
the Southern California weather
like living in a time loop
with no hope of escape.

As a member of the leadership team
I'm supposed to mingle
in the crowds,
make newcomers feel welcome

although sometimes
I'm excused
from this introvert's nightmare

not because anyone cares
about my spoons

but because I'm preparing
for a performance I will give
during the programming.

There is
at least
some respect
for my craft.

At 7:17
the overhead lights go off
fog machine on
loud techno music
fills the space

                        the opening notes of
                        "Get Ready for This"
                        a surefire trigger.

Brett throws open the door
from his office and bounds onto the stage

      (it's only the front of the portable
      but the production is slick
      and it feels like a stage
      and he feels like a star)

and I watch as four flimsy walls
shake with the energy of one hundred teenagers
screaming and cheering for him

and I know
I'm the one
he wants behind closed doors.

I attended Brett's Edge
every Sunday
for three years

not only attended
but planned, programmed
participated
in the running of things

and even though
I can remember
in exact detail
what I was wearing
the first time Brett took me
to his apartment alone

where we were in his office
the first time
he pushed me onto my knees
and held my head
where he wanted it

what bus seat
I sat on
while he called me
a whore

I have only a vague sense
of what happened at the Edge.

I remember the music
the lights
some programming
a talk.
Dissociation
is a powerful drug.

I ask some friends
what happened
at the Edge
and their responses
unleash a tidal wave
of memories
that nearly drown me.

Slickly produced
videos with no purpose but fun
high-tech skits
though sometimes
the skits are live

often based on pop culture
like the one that parodies
the scene in *Forrest Gump*
where Jenny plays guitar naked
but the girl in our skit wears a bikini
and plays guitar, looking naked
at a church event

and I don't wish
it had been a purity-culture
kind of church where girls couldn't
show their shoulders
but also
maybe
a teenage girl
shouldn't have been asked
to do that for laughs.

I'm not the kind of girl
who plays guitar
semi-naked for laughs.

I'm the kind of girl
who writes serious monologues
on serious issues
some of which
I'm grappling with
at the time

        eating disorders
        self-harm
        suicide
        peer pressure

                (though I'm never
                asked to write a monologue
                about when your youth pastor
                puts his hand
                down your pajama pants
                at a church retreat)

and performs them
for the same group
who has just hooted and hollered
at the nearly naked girl in the bikini

or a gross-out game
like eating melted candy bars
out of diapers and identifying them

or a group of boys
doing a lip-synch
to a Boyz II Men song

and then I stand up there
and bare
my split-open
heart.

I, who make my life of words,
cannot fathom
adequate ones
to convey
how furious I am

that this was
essentially
my first experience
as a playwright.

There's one monologue
that's so personal

      probably
      on eating disorders
      but I can't remember

that I get so anxious
I make myself sick
and fret in Brett's office
while kids are arriving
and I'm supposed to be mingling,
making other people comfortable

and I tell Brett
when he passes through the office
that I don't think I can perform this one
I really don't want to do it

and he says
this is my responsibility
it's already in the programming
I don't have a choice.

      Buck up, Joy.

Part of me wishes
I still had those monologues

early juvenilia
of someone
who would go on
to pour all my rage
into words
that fill so many
books and plays

but they are lost
to time
to an early '90s computer with no cloud
to an age without backups
to my parents' divorce

when my bedroom full
of links to those days
stuffed in desk drawers
and on bookshelves
would be packed away
or mostly discarded
while I was at college.

I didn't write
creatively, of my own accord.
Not in high school.

I had, as a child
but by my teenage years
I was too busy
getting straight As
in advanced classes
too busy devoting every moment
to Brett and his demands

it never would have occurred to me
to spend a second
on writing for myself.

I get my driver's license
just before junior year
because school is a twenty-minute drive away
and there are no buses for the high school.

But within a couple weeks
I get in an accident

        minor, my fault

and that is reason enough
to hold off driving again
losing my freedom
for another six months.

JUNIOR YEAR

When you live in San Diego
you go somewhere even hotter
to retreat from cool ocean breezes
which is how the youth groups ends up
going to Palm Springs my junior year.

This one's for the whole group,
not just the leadership team,
which means staying at a conference center
and not someone's living room.

I'm on Meg's bed while she packs—
sunscreen, bathing suit, shorts, and tank tops
and a floral romper, playful and fun,
nothing like I'd usually wear.

That's so cute.

She tosses it to me.

       You should wear it!

I wave her off but she insists
I try it on. So I do.
The girl in the mirror
is breezy, no earthly concerns,
exactly who I want to be,
if only for a weekend.

I leave it on
a little self-conscious
and we head for church.

The youth group van
pulls into a grocery store
halfway to Palm Springs
for snacks and cold drinks.

The desert heat slams into me
as soon as the door slides open.

The van will be an oven within minutes
so I go inside the store.
I won't buy anything, though.
That would be almost as bad
as eating in front of people,
which I never do.

I separate from the group
and head for the freezer aisle
just to feel the cool air on my skin
before it's back into the suffocating heat.

   What are you wearing?

Brett's breath on my neck is hot
as he materializes behind me.

   You're showing everything.

I'm really not, no more skin
than the other girls
dressed for the desert heat.
I think I look cute.
I look fun.

     I looked young.

This isn't
Jesus-cries-when-you-show-your-shoulders
purity-culture bullshit—
it's never been that kind of youth group.
Girls (not me) will wear bikinis
at the pool when we arrive
and the leaders won't care.

You look like a slut.

I change
at the retreat center
into a T-shirt, modest shorts.
Meg asks why. I shrug.

I was sweaty from the drive.

I'm supposed to update
the boys next door
about the evening schedule.

I walk into a room full of guys
I've known for years. Fellow SALT members,
a few freshmen. They're rambunctious,
no one's listening to me.

I finally make them pay attention,
scold them like a mom, because
I'm always the responsible one.
They recite the schedule back.
I turn to leave, when someone says,

Do it!

Two boys jump up
and freak on me—a dance move
that simulates sex, hips thrusting
till they double over laughing
at the hilarity of sexualizing me,
the straitlaced pastor's daughter.

My fury is white-hot
over a few seconds
of stupid immaturity.

I want to scream at them
claw their eyes out

because they are a safe target
for my rage
at having my body
made a thing
for someone else's
amusement.

I don't scream
or rage
or show any cracks
in my above-it-all facade.

I hold my head up
haughty
and stalk from the room
while they laugh behind me

and another drop of fury
is added to the cauldron.

A few different churches
have come together for this retreat
and the next day we choose
between sessions with the various leaders.

I go to Brett's because
of what would happen if I didn't

    you look like a slut

and because everyone is
going to Brett's talk.
He's the coolest, the funniest,
and they can't wait to hear
what he'll say on this particular topic:
                                            sex.

The presence
of other youth leaders
around this retreat
means Brett hasn't spoken to me
since the grocery store.

There is relief in no contact
but also
I know things will only be worse
when we are finally alone.

I find a seat
against the wall
of a packed room
and listen to him tell us
with humor and relatable language
about stumbling blocks

and slippery slopes,
how true love waits
and masturbation is a sin
and sex within marriage
is the best.

(His wife's not here.)

I can't help but notice
he never looks my way.

True Love Waits?
The Radiohead song?

my editor asks
and no, even before
the first performance
of that song
there was an abstinence movement
with pledges to sign
and rings engraved with the words

    true love waits

to be worn on your left hand
often given to a girl by her father
in a special ceremony
and worn until replaced
by your husband

and our church didn't go that far
we were lucky
Brett was cooler than that

but it was there
the culture we might slip into
if Brett wasn't there to keep us edgy.

Brett preaches
about the slippery slope
of physical intimacy.

Once you've crossed one line
you'll always go at least that far
and even farther.

There's a metaphor
about calluses
in there somewhere.
I've blocked out the details.

Our youth group
hasn't kissed dating goodbye.
In fact, at overnights
dating SALT members
snuggle next to each other
in sleeping bags
under Brett's
(distracted) supervision.

He's the cool adult
who's been there, who gets it.
I wonder if I'm the only one
who notices
he never delineates
the line.

Christians
are not a monolith.

Our warped views
on sex
are a spectrum

from those who believe
one shouldn't even kiss
until marriage

to those who believe
it's pretty much a free-for-all
as long as a penis
doesn't go inside a vagina
you're good
you're still virgins
you're not cheating

you're definitely not
raping a child.

I am fifteen.
I am sixteen
I am seventeen.

      A child
      to me now
      as I watch
      my own children
      hit those ages,
      growing into their adulthood
      but nowhere near it, truly.

A child to the law.
A person under eighteen
in California
cannot consent to sex.

Brett tells me
my body
is a woman's

    and so
    I try to starve
    myself back into a child.

Some years after college
I see an article
written by a youth pastor
convicted of abusing a child in his care.

He refers to his victim
as his friend
and the abuse
as an extramarital relationship.
The focus of the article
is on grace for him
with no voice for the victim.

My online comment pointing this out
      as well as other comments
      by other survivors
is deleted by *Christianity Today*.

A friend helps me place an article
on a smaller, faith-based website
      now defunct,
      the article another lost bit of
          ephemera
where I write directly
for the first time
about my abuse.

Another first,
I call it
what it was: rape.

And in the comments
someone tells me
that because I was a teen

because I drove myself there
because I waited years to speak up

it wasn't really rape.
In fact
they say
they hope
one day
I'm really raped
so I know the difference.

Rape culture
tells us
rape
is a stranger
in an alley
with a knife or a gun

the woman screaming, fighting for her life
as he forces sex organ into sex organ.

But if instead
he uses fingers or an object
       is that somehow less invasive?

If it's not an alley
but instead a bedroom
or a church office
       is that somehow less terrorizing?

If it's not a stranger
but instead a friend, a relative,
a pastor, a teacher, a coach
       is that somehow less horrifying?

If it's not a knife or gun
but instead a promise
of desperately sought affection
or the threat of his suicide
or the coercion of his authority
is that somehow less traumatic?

If it's not one nightmarish event
but instead three years
of carving away at a girl

belittling her, manipulating her,
isolating her
until she is starving
and slicing herself open
and planning how to die

is that somehow less violent?

A story like this
involves so many people
some of whom should feel guilt
                              but don't
and some who were only kids themselves
but later express their guilt and sadness
their feeling that they should have spoken up
when things seemed off
when Brett spent too much time with me.

       Carter tells me later
       he confronted Brett once,
       told him he didn't think
       it was appropriate
       for him to spend so much time
           with me.

       Brett said he had to act
       as a father figure to me
       because my own father
       was so absent

       never mind
       that my father
       was nearly always
       grappling with his own demons
       in the next building over

and I have to refocus
again and again
on my right to tell my story

and I know that it matters because
Artemisia learned from Judith and Susanna

and I learned from Artemisia
and readers learned from *Blood Water Paint*
and went on to tell their own stories,
share their own rage
get their own justice.

My father's demons
give me pause.
Is it my story to tell
that while Brett pushed me to my knees
in the portable office

over in the main building
my senior pastor father
was abusing his own power
with women under his authority?

He'll call it infidelity
        that *happened in tandem with love*
in his own memoir.
The San Francisco Presbytery
will call it sexual abuse.
They're women his age
but he has spiritual authority

                not to mention
                he's their boss.

That's all his story
except when it bleeds into mine
when he won't hold to account
another man for sexual indiscretions
he's all too familiar with

and there seems to be a theme
of blurred lines and boundless grace
and removing the plank from one's own eye
before calling out the speck in another's
but if you never remove the plank
it's just the blind leading the blind.

Brett gives me the code
to get into his apartment building
so I never have to linger
outside
where I might be seen

and instead let myself in
and slip up the back stairs
never the elevator
because the stairwell
is right next to his apartment door
so there's less chance I'll be seen

the only thing is
they have a neighbor
across the hall
a single woman
who's friendly with his wife
and home during the day

so when he knows I'm coming
    (and he always knows,
      I'm always summoned)
he hovers by his door
watching and waiting
so that if she comes out
he can throw his door open
and chat loudly with her,
while I wait in the stairwell
until she goes back inside

because I can't be seen.

He only pushes me
onto my back on the couch
                            once
because after that
he always takes me
directly to the bedroom.

I try to connect.
That's why I'm there.

Can we talk?

        Later.
        I want you so much.

He might not be listening
but I have his undivided attention.
That's why I let this happen,
I don't scream or fight,
I don't tell anyone,
because there's always the chance
he'll listen to me before
I'm on my back

                except he never does

or maybe at least he'll listen after
when he's sweeping the bed clear
of my long, straight hairs,
so different from his wife's tight curls

but after
he only ever wants
to shove me
                out the door.

When I bring my charges forward
not only to the police
but to my friends from high school
and the church I grew up in

I call it sexual abuse.

That's not inaccurate.

But also
it leaves so much room
for people to fill in
their preferred version.

It could mean "only" kissing

> in itself sexual abuse
> between an adult authority and a minor
> but if you really want
> to forgive him
> you could justify
> call it bad judgment
> call him immature
> move past it

or it could mean
complete nudity
digital penetration
oral sex
hand jobs
ejaculation on my body

which is what it was.

Sex ed
in the '90s
is laughable
but I know enough
to understand
that if semen gets inside
my body
it could fertilize an egg
resulting in pregnancy

and while he never
crosses that one final line
he does ejaculate
and then shove fingers up
so hard I drive home bleeding

and every moment
until my next period comes
I quietly panic
while leading Bible study
while taking an AP test
while setting the table

that enough of him
could be inside me
to fertilize an egg.

Brett is loud
in his opposition
to abortion.

Killing babies
        and a fertilized egg
        would be a baby
        immediately
is murder.

My parents are the kind of Christians
who believe Jesus's whole deal
was caring for the poor and oppressed.
But they're quiet on abortion.
It's a land mine in the church.

I've never heard of Planned Parenthood.

                Later I'd learn some girls
                went to Tijuana for abortions.
                I was in driving distance of the border
                but this never would have occurred to me
                and I would have had to go
                                alone.

If I am pregnant
I will swallow
the bottle of pills
in my nightstand.

If my mother finds them
like she found my diet pills
I will say they're
to help me sleep

but I haven't taken a single one
because I will need
the whole bottle
if it comes to that.

Later
I'll read
about abuse survivors
who feel pleasure

and then shame
at that pleasure

confusion
that they must have wanted it
if their bodies responded.

I feel shame
        so much shame
at being so desperate
for affection, for attention

but my body
protects me
from ever associating
this man with pleasure.

I feel nothing.
I leave my body.

This is a gift.

But also

it is a long

                slow

                              process

       later

                      to learn

      to allow

             my body

                         to feel pleasure.

In college
an older boyfriend
not raised in purity culture
wants more than I'll give
but he never pushes further.

Without question
he follows strange rules I concoct,
ways to make me feel safe
when we're on a bed together.

The boundaries
are more about how he'll respond
than a particular moral line
and I'm astonished
when he respects them.

He won't have fun
if I'm not having fun.
                        Which seems obvious now
                        but was a revelation then.

He touches me
out of desire
but also for my pleasure
and it's like I've never
done any of this before
because I haven't.

I haven't.

I've never been
inside my body
feeling the hands
of someone who
wants to hear
how they make me feel

who cares
how I feel
at all.

Brett's gotten
what he wanted
when a key turns in the lock.

(His wife's work schedule is firm;
she's never home in the afternoon
but she's the only one with a key.)

She doesn't come
straight to the bedroom
which gives Brett the chance
to throw me and my clothes
into the bathroom
and when I emerge
she sees the back of my head
as he shoves me out the door.

Joy just came by to borrow a CD.

She had to know.
Didn't she?

After all
the meet-cute they share is
she was a high school student
while he was a youth group volunteer.
But then again, I know what it's like

to want to believe you're special,
that this isn't a pattern, a grasp for power,
that he's never done anything like this before
and never will again, but it's different with you
because he loves you that much.

My mother knew
about the other women
but also my father told her
she was delusional
so many times
she eventually believed it

her belief in her own instincts
shattered like the glass trinkets,
gifts from his mistress,
that she threw out the window
onto a stone patio
when she finally reached her breaking point

and he made her clean up the shards herself.

I'm on my period
so surely this time
we'll only talk

except it makes no difference
it's all the same
his fingers drive

the tampon farther
up and in
than it's ever gone before.

At home, I'm frantic.
I can't find the string,
can't feel the tampon.

What happens
when something
is pushed farther
than it was ever meant to go?

I'm so panicked
I call him
from my home phone to his
even though
my mom is home
his wife is home.

I'm crying,
trying to explain
the emergency.
I'm mortified
but what other adult
can I turn to?

I don't remember
his exact words.
I do remember
his response was
                    cruel and belittling.

Something along the lines of,

      Why are you being such a baby?

I get invited
to take an acting class
for advanced students
at the university
which meets on Sunday afternoons
for six weeks.

I'll be able to go to morning service
and I'll be back in time for the Edge
but I'll miss some of the SALT meeting
that happens from 5:00 to 7:00.

When I ask Brett
if this will work
he is angry
I would even consider
an activity that would keep me
from my responsibilities to him
to the church.

Never mind
that I am a junior,
a high-achieving student
aiming for the best colleges
where I plan to study theater
and become an actor.

This is an incredible opportunity,
one an adult who wants the best for me
should support and encourage.

But Brett wants
what's best for him,
which is me at his side
where he can see me
where he can control me
every moment.

I do the class.

                                I don't remember
                                the fallout.

                                Perhaps
                                I called his bluff

                                or perhaps
                                it was so bad
                                my brain protects me.

I go away
the summer before
my senior year
to a theater program
at the college I hope to attend

a program
I set my sights on
as a freshman
before Brett even arrived

worked hard
saving money
for three years
to pay my way

so his disapproval
couldn't keep me home

and suddenly
I am two thousand miles away
with only a landline
in a shared dorm room
to tether me to Brett

and my schedule is so busy
with daytime classes
        mostly for acting
        but I choose
        a writing elective too

and nighttime rehearsals
        for *Medea*
        in which I play the nurturing Nurse

>   but thrill to the furious woman
>   at the center of the story, her rage
>   and ruthless action
>   at a world of men
>   who would deny her

I am barely
in touch with Brett
and can finally breathe
which is wild because
I didn't even know
I was suffocating.

Sometime during the summer program
I get a cold
and miss a day of classes and rehearsals.

I'm shut up in the dorm room,
loopy on cold medicine,
when Brett calls.

                         Did he call every day,
                         or was it mere coincidence
                         that he found me this one day
                         I was in the room?

I'm away from home,
sick without my mother
for the first time,
so hearing from someone
who cares about me
is nice
        for a second.

        Who's that?
        In the background?

There's no one
in the dorm at all.
Everyone else is in class.

        There's someone in your room.

I'm alone.

        There's a guy.
        I can hear his voice.
        You have a guy in your room.

My head pounds.
My thoughts blur.
He yells for a while.

The cold medicine
pulls me under.

I return
to San Diego
to him

but I've had a glimpse
of what life might be like
if it didn't revolve
around him

and the hourglass
of his grip on me
starts running out of sand.

Dear Ann,

Putnams have a long history as storytellers. Your descendants will go on to found a publishing house. In fact, this very book will be published by the same conglomerate that owns G. P. Putnam's Sons (not daughters). But that's not why I feel a connection to your story.

Your friend Elizabeth was sent away by her parents to avoid the rising hysteria in Salem, like my sister went away to college. You must have felt the loss, as I did. But also, like I filled a role I didn't even know my sister had been playing, you saw your chance to take your place next to brassy, confident Abigail.

You saw your chance to raise your voice.

But it wasn't your voice, exactly, was it? It wasn't your story. Your father was the scribe, writing the court documents and shaping the testimony. He fed you names. So did your mother. They needed you to fulfill their petty adult grievances over land and money and power.

They noticed you.

Your parents hadn't noticed you in years, not with so many younger brothers and sisters. And then Baby Sarah was born cold and blue. That fool Arthur Miller decided your mother required seven stillborn babies in order to be driven to senseless accusations of witchcraft, but you knew one dead baby was enough.

And then your parents died, shortly after the trials, leaving you, nineteen years old, to care for eight siblings. With the weight of all that had happened, you wouldn't make it to forty. Fourteen years after the name Salem became synonymous with hysterical girls, you stood before the congregation of the same church you'd grown up in—oh, those places of childhood worship—and confessed your sins from all those years before.

You'd been made an instrument for the accusing of several persons of a grievous crime; you now had grounds to believe they were innocent persons and it was a great delusion of Satan; that you had brought upon yourself and your land the guilt of innocent blood.

You were the only one to confess among your friends, but also the townsfolk. While countless adults flung accusations forgotten by history, you were the lone accuser to admit what you must have grappled with every time you closed your eyes, every time you saw a dead animal or a broomstick. Or a hanging.

I hope, somewhere in those hard-backed pews, amidst the guilt and penance, that you felt somewhere, somehow the slightest bit of compassion for the impressionable young girl you were.

We were both so young, Ann.

Ann Putnam Jr.
(1679–1716, Salem, MA)
Ann was one of the most prolific of the Salem accusers. Her father was the primary scribe of the court proceedings. She is the only Salem accuser who later apologized for her actions.

SENIOR
YEAR

Senior year
means college applications
and I've known where I'm going
      or at least hoping to
since freshman year
when I learned
about Northwestern University's
renowned theater program.

    But how can you go so far away?

I apply to one Christian school
in Seattle, which I've always loved

to UC San Diego
to placate Brett

        and UC Davis
        which I don't tell him

        because if it turns out
        I need a safety
        there's no way I'm staying
        in San Diego.

I've never gone
on the annual ski trip
because I don't ski
or care to learn
and can't afford it

but Brett decides
I am required
as a SALT member
even though
there will be no SALT responsibilities.

I know it will be
Palm Springs all over
except this time
everything will be frozen
tight as my chest
every time I try
to breathe in Brett's presence.

No other SALT members
have their way paid
in exchange for services
and leadership.

    Don't tell the others.

It's an eight-hour drive
to the ski resort in Utah
so instead of Brett driving the van
the church charters a bus.

The week before
is a flurry of planning
who will sit with whom.

The youth group is our social center
and even when it's not an organized activity
we hang out at Brett's house
at Chili's with Brett
always with Brett

so school
is the only time
with no Brett around.

> (He assistant coaches
> the wrestling team
> so he sometimes appears at lunch
> but class time is safe.)

Over junior and senior year
I've gotten close to Logan,
who attends youth group activities
but whose parents don't attend the church.
He's a massive flirt
with no expectations of me.
He's fun. We laugh, we joke,
we're affectionate.

We exchange mixtapes

and have long phone conversations
and I entertain fantasies
of being a normal teen.

>   *You've never even been kissed,*
>   Logan teases me
>   on the phone

and what do I say to that
when I've probably done more
      had more done to me
than even flirty Logan has.

>   Though I came to understand that
>   just as rape is not sex, but violence,
>   when Brett shoved his mouth against mine
>   it wasn't ever a kiss
>   with the mutual affection
>   implied in the word.
>
>   Perhaps even with everything
>   that had happened
>   Logan was right
>   and I still hadn't
>   truly
>   been kissed.

Yes, I have.

>   *What are you talking about?*
>   *Who?*

I can't tell him the truth.

At the summer program
I went to.
I had a boyfriend.

I didn't.

Brett gets wind
of my flirtation with Logan
and punishes him.
Doesn't accept him
into SALT when he applies.

Tells me Logan
is a player
and it's true
that he flirts
with several girls at a time
but he's honest about it,
always clear about who he is.

We're at school
when Logan asks
if I'll sit with him
on the bus to Utah

and free of Brett's oppressive gaze
I think for a minute
this fantasy with Logan
could really happen.

I say yes.

I avoid Brett
as we mill in the parking lot,
boarding the bus. He hasn't asked
who I'm sitting with.
He assumes I'll save him
a seat. It's unspoken.

I'm wearing a bracelet
Logan gave me for Christmas—
silver drama masks linked in a chain.

                        He got a bracelet that Christmas
                        from the same mall kiosk for another girl.
                        Hers was hearts or flowers or something.
                        I didn't care.
                        He thought of what I'd like.

We sit together
in the back half
on the left side
                        details etched in my brain
                        like cheap tragedy masks
and when Brett climbs onto the bus
his gaze lasers on me.

I'm by the window,
Logan's basketball-player frame
a shield from what's coming
but he's no match for Brett's control.

Switch seats
with me, Logan.

It isn't a request.
Still, Logan looks to me,
a question in his eyes.

                                What if I'd told him not to?
                                Insisted Logan stay.
                                Right then
                                with all those people around,
                                what would Brett have done?

But I'm not there yet.

            I need to talk to Joy.
            SALT stuff.

It's not SALT stuff
he hisses into my ear
as I sit trapped against the window
for the endless drive.

whore
slut
ungrateful
duty
love
betrayal
slut
whore

At the ski lodge
I'm assigned to a room with younger girls,
their counselor, so wise.

>*You're so mature*
>a constant refrain.

No other adults
have come on this trip.
Only Brett.

With our first evening free,
my friends put on bikinis,
San Diego girls excited to sink
into a hot tub while snow
melts into the water,
insubstantial as my voice.

I'm not as comfortable
in a bathing suit as the others,
obsessed as I've become
with taking up less and less space,
exercising compulsively
living on rice cakes and diet soda
horrified by any hint of curve
that might catch the eye, his eye.

But these moments of feeling
like a regular teen
are so fleeting.
Logan's bracelet
on my wrist a reminder
of the possibilities.
I put on my one-piece suit,

follow my giddy group of friends
down the hall of the resort.

We're almost to the exit
when a door opens,
Brett stepping out of his room.

    Joy. SALT stuff.

I clutch a beach wrap
around my bathing suit
inside Brett's room.

He's all caresses
and apologies
for the invectives on the bus.

> *I'm sorry*
> *you upset me.*

He just loves me so much.
Logan doesn't care about me.
But I must not love him
if I could wound him like that.
Maybe it would be better
if he weren't here,
if he ended his life
and let me live mine.

Somehow
his apologies
turn into mine.

How can he say such a thing?
Think such a thing?
He does so much good,
means so much
to so many—

> *But not to you.*
> *And you're the only one*
> *who matters.*

I show him
he matters to me
on my knees.

When I'm certain
I've saved his life
(for tonight)

and he's sure
I'm fully devoted
(forever)

I finally meet my friends
at the hot tub
where I slip into the water
quick as I can
before someone comments
on my shrinking body

and try to ignore
the coating in my mouth
down my throat
a constant reminder
that I am not
one of these girls.

Later, when I peel off
the clinging suit
I notice the brilliant silver
of the linked drama masks
has vanished in the alchemy
of the hot tub and transformed
to a dull, worn tarnish.

There's no question
who I sit with
on the bus ride home.

I don't fight it.
By the time
we pull into the church lot
at one in the morning
I only want to be home
in my own bed
where I might not sleep
but no one can
make demands of me.

I slip away from Brett
while he unlocks the portable
for those kids who need
to call their parents.

Logan offers to drive me home.
I climb in, so grateful
to escape without a fuss.
He's putting my bag in the back
when my passenger door opens.

   You have to stay.

Brett's there, too close,
fury in his eyes.

   You're here as a leader.

All around us
other SALT members
climb into cars.
Logan climbs into the driver's side.

This is the moment I replay

      over and over
                      over and over
            over and over
                         a skipping record.

    What if I'd made a different choice here?

No, Brett. I'm done.
Logan, let's go.

        Except
        that's not what happened.

        But
              what if

        it was?

His eyes flash
disbelief at my rebellion.

    Come on, Joy.
    Don't worry about her, Logan.
    I'll get her home.

And Logan waits for my decision
because it's my decision, isn't it?
I'm almost eighteen.
I'm so *mature*.

      What would have been different

         could have been
              different
     if I'd told Logan to drive

    drive drive drive drive drive
    away from here
    please just go now
    he'll let go
    of the door
    he'll let go

                     Logan was just enough outside
                                      outside
          of Brett's orbit that he would have

he will
if I ask
if I speak up

                he would have he would have
          if I'd had the guts
                        to leave Brett standing there

              guts churning, turning

    and then there'd be no turning back for me

no turning back, no turning back
    (I have decided to follow Jesus)

          we'd get to my house and sit in the driveway
          where I'd tell Logan about that first SALT retreat
          about the apartment code and the stairwell

          I'd tell Logan about the office
          about the ski lodge about the threats about the
              promises

                I'd tell Logan
                and then I'd know what it felt like to tell someone

Logan's just a kid
he can't do anything but

                        then I'd have told someone.
                              I'd know how that felt

                        to tell someone

                                to tell someone

                                        to tell someone

                    and I'd have no choice
                    but to go inside and tell my mother

                        could I tell my mother?
                        did I know even then
                              before I knew anything
                            about my sister
                    that my dad wouldn't help

and I explode his world before he has the chance to build up his defense
    and cover his tracks and lay the groundwork and call me

                  that crazy girl

                          crazy girl   crazy girl   crazy girl
                  she'll come telling stories
                  but she's unwell
                  it's sad, really

None of that happens.
I get out of Logan's car
and follow Brett dutifully
to the portable
where I wait
for the others
to get picked up
by parents who know
and care where they are
in the middle of the night.

I have decided to follow Brett
but something is different this time.

> I'd like to say that when
> the bracelet tarnished
> in the hot tub
> I had a poetic revelation
> about abuse masquerading as love
> but that was life
> handing me a metaphor
> I wouldn't see until later.
>
> So many things
> I wouldn't see
> until later.

But in this moment
I am done.
I haven't gotten out
of the car to let Brett
cajole and threaten
and push me to my knees.

When the last car pulls out of the lot
and only his pickup remains
there I am, alone with him
in an abandoned church
in the middle of the night.

> (How did no one see?)

He starts in.
I'm ungrateful/slutty/cruel/all he ever needed.

I just want to go home.

I don't follow the script this time,
follow him down the path
where his apologies turn into mine,
where his threats turn into my actions.

I just want to go home.

This revision to the dialogue
throws him. Losing control
angers him, endangers me.

                He never hit me, but if he had
                it would have been that night.

Instead he turns up the declarations of love,
how he's never loved anyone as much
as he loves me, he'll divorce his wife
as soon as he's able (my eighteenth birthday
just weeks away) he'll die without me.

I just want to go home.

                It's poetic to repeat the refrain,
                but I wasn't that resolute.
                I was done, yes, but also human,
                also an exhausted child.
                I engaged as I always did
                with the magic words,
                the specter of suicide
                not understanding until so much later
                that he would never do it,
                it was only a form of control
                and not even an original one.

His life is too valuable
never mind that I keep
a bottle of sleeping pills
in my bedside table.

I plead with him
for his life, tell him I can't
do this anymore but
it doesn't mean
I don't love him.

I just want to go home.

Finally he drives me home.
What else can he do?
We cannot go in circles through the night
until church staff show up in the morning.
I have no curfew
because if I'm with the youth pastor
obviously I'm safe
but if I didn't come home at all
surely someone would notice?

      I have replayed this night
      so many times because
      it feels like a pivotal moment
      if I'd only handled it differently

      but I haven't thought until now
      until this writing
      about what that night was like
      for him, as he drove away.

      It could be his arrogance,
      his practice in controlling girls like me
      made him overconfident,
      sure I'd be back
      at his feet
      the next day

      but I don't think so.

      This was different.
      I'd never denied him before.
      Never stood up for myself.
      Never told him I was done.

Did he worry about
what I'd do, who I'd tell?
Did he panic,
begin to lay groundwork then?
Did he, at the very least,
have a single sleepless night
at the prospect
of
consequences?

In a world
before social media
and cell phones
it's simpler to make a break.
He can only call my home phone
(his boss's home phone)
so many times.
He can't leave
anguished messages.

Simpler, but not easy
for the pastor's daughter
whose world has revolved
around youth group
for three and a half years,
to suddenly make a break
with one semester left.

Sunday mornings are impossible
to avoid—there would be too many questions
if I stopped going to church entirely
but I quit SALT,
stay away from Bible studies and the Edge,
from social hangouts
that include Brett (which is all of them).

People notice.
        (Though not my parents.)
How could they not?

        Brett and Joy had a fight.

It's grotesque.
He's not my boyfriend,
but everyone acts
like this is a breakup.

He bemoans my cruelty,
how I'm *wounding* him.
People take sides.

Perhaps it's because
I'll soon be gone to college
but I find for the first time
I don't care
what people think.

He's always covered his tracks
with such precision
it's almost like
he's done this before.

Notes oblique, never
writes the things he says aloud.
Mixtapes full of love songs
are no big deal—he makes them
for everyone (but mine are different).

But on Valentine's Day
two weeks after the ski trip
he parks on the cul-de-sac above my house
so his truck won't be seen
by any passersby,
sneaks down with flowers
he leaves on the doorstep
when he knows
I'm home alone.

I watch him through the living room window
where I once watched my sister
climb into his truck
and thought I was jealous.

Dear Gertrud,

All you wanted was to be loved. It's the heart of all these stories, isn't it?

But just because you were Sven's daughter—it was right there in your name, like a brand burned into your skin, Svensdotter—it didn't mean your father could meet your needs. He tried, in his way. With your mother dead, he wanted to offer you a maternal figure, someone who could be what you needed. And you loved the maid Märet, almost like a mother. She would do for a wife, he thought. Then you'd have what you needed.

But Märet left you both, ran off to toil as some other man's wife, and care for some other child.

Only eight years old, you were bounced from house to house, family members allowing you in and shuffling you along with alarming frequency. You must have wondered what you were doing wrong. Why did your story insist on the constant refrain of people leaving you, or shoving you out the door?

At your aunt's house, it was a cruel joke that you were meant to mind the sheep. All day long devoted to keeping the helpless creatures secure in their home, making sure they didn't leave, only to return to your bed and hope you'd still be welcome there.

When that shepherd boy began edging his flock closer to yours, you were cold and your feet ached. You tried to give him the hint that he shouldn't distract you.

When he edged closer still, your flocks intermingling, you fumed. You weren't going to mess this up, lose your place again.

And when you punched him, it was instinct. Twelve years was old enough for you to know where he shouldn't put his hands. But not to anticipate how he'd make you pay.

Gertrud Svensdotter is a witch! he proclaimed.

Only by witchcraft could you have walked across the water like he said you did, leading your sheep away, out of his reach. Only by witchcraft could you deny him what he wanted.

Admit it, the priests told you, and twelve years was old enough for you to know you must listen to church authorities. Old enough to know the truth didn't matter anyway. Old enough to know someone had to pay for a boy's wounded pride.

But who to blame for the accusations against you? Your mother was dead. You could have blamed your father. But if you did that, you'd be slamming the door on the chance that he might ever take you back. Instead you blamed the one who left, who could have stayed and given you a home. Who had almost as little power as you did, which meant she was vulnerable, which meant you might be believed.

Märet Jonsdotter led me to the devil, you said.

You couldn't have known how it would snowball. Would you have said it if you did? Your impulse turned into an avalanche, the Swedish countryside blanketed in a blizzard of accusations flying against Märet, against you, against anyone in the way but if you kept talking, kept accusing, you were helpful. Not guilty.

Or at least more helpful than guilty.

When you were flogged for your transgressions—which transgressions?— the welts faded, but as stark in your memory as blood on snow would be the sound of heads falling as eight people, including Märet, lost their lives because a boy put his hands on you and you would not have it.

And really, that's on him. But history doesn't take kindly to girls who fight back, Gertrud. Believe me, I know.

Gertrud Svensdotter
(1656–1675, Sweden)
Gertrud was a twelve-year-old Swedish girl who had an altercation with a shepherd boy. Later he claimed he'd seen her walk on water. Encouraged by a priest to admit it, Gertrud claimed a woman named Märet Jonsdotter had "led her to the devil," which kicked off the witch trials in Sweden.

I go to build houses in Mexico
over spring break because
it's the one trip I love
and Brett will not take it from me.

Enough months have passed
since the ski trip, the flowers,
that he's stopped calling,
stopped pushing,
maybe started to believe
I meant it when I said
never again.

Another gathering
in the church parking lot
as we load our bags
and take seats in the van
but this time—
        for the first time
I don't sit up front.

I've just received
what I've been waiting for—
my acceptance letter
to Northwestern University.

I tell my friends.
They cheer, knowing
it's what I've been working toward.

And all the way to Mexico,
Brett drives with tears
tracking down his face,
gazing mournfully at me

in the rearview mirror,
sad songs on repeat.

                        Everyone knew
                        what he was crying about.
                        How did no one
                        question how inappropriate that was?

In Mexico
Ethan asks me to prom.
He's a good friend
whose greatest rebellion
is sneaking out of his house
to go to Bible study,
which his parents disapprove of.
They're not church people
and they're disturbed
by what they hear
of the youth group.

Ethan is kind, smart,
funny, sensitive—so I say yes.
I've never been to a school dance.

> So many things I've never done
> either because I've been
> constrained by Brett's obsessive control
> or had some twisted version thrust upon me.

When prom night comes
our big group meets for photos
at a palatial home
and Brett is there, eyes on me
and my wisp of a frame
in a purple halter dress, a string of pearls.

> *Why was he at your prom photos?*
> my editor asks
> and it's never occurred to me
> that was odd.
> I cannot overstate
> how he was everywhere

             he was the center
             always
             even at something
             that had nothing to do
             with church, with him.

I avoid Brett's gaze, pose with friends,
hold on to Ethan's sturdy arm,
lightheaded from hunger.

By some miracle
Brett doesn't join us for dinner
at a fancy restaurant
         (where I don't eat, I never eat)
but when we reach the dance
he's there as a chaperone.

Chaperones: present
to prevent anything untoward.

I'm frail, weakened
by a bout with mono
and my undernourished body,
so I sit out the fast dances
while Ethan dotes on me.
When a slow dance comes, though,
I can't find him.

He's been cornered outside
by a morose Brett,
who monopolizes my prom date
to mope about my cruelty.
He's worried about my walk with God,
he's worried about my eating disorder
         (he's worried about himself).

It's not until halfway through
the last dance of the night
that Ethan breaks away from him,
comes to hold me in arms
so much gentler than Brett's ever been
and we sway to "Lady in Red."

PART II

COLLEGE

The first time
I tell someone
I call it an affair.

I sit in another hot tub,
this time no snow
but an evening breeze
at April's condo
during our first summer
home from college.

We're children
in that churning water
but we feel so adult,
finally free from the restraints
of teenage years.

I didn't come over
planning to tell her.
But April has noticed
I haven't folded back into Brett's orbit
this first summer after college.

I've stayed far away
from our high school friends.
I'm working at a theater
on the other side of town,
dating an actor
unconnected to our social group

who continue to flit
around Brett's blazing-hot bulb.

              I don't remember
              how Brett came up.
              Probably we were gossiping
              about mutual friends
              from youth group.

              Maybe she asked
              if I ever talked to him
              anymore, or what happened
              at the end of senior year.

April knows what Brett was like with me.
She was there all along
at SALT meetings
and retreats and ski trips.
She knows what he was like.

              Nothing physical ever happened
              between them but
              she told me years later
              that she'd felt the possibility.
              Her mom couldn't understand
              why Brett called her so much,
              why she said *I love you*
              at the end of each call.

                  (Everyone had to, or he'd be angry.
                  At least the girls. We just accepted it.
                  I didn't realize until later
                  that he didn't spend hours on the phone
                  with the guys, didn't demand
                  their declarations of love.)

She's shocked
and not
when I tell her.
It's the most horrifying thing
and the most obvious,
all churned up in the water between us.

I'm still not calling it abuse.
I was old enough
to handle AP classes
and college applications
and professional acting.
He didn't force me.

Did he?

Dear Geillis,

Your story involves some of the most powerful, revered men in history. But no one knows your name today.

I'm guessing your master didn't know your name even then. He certainly didn't know you were Gilly to your friends. Your master, David Seton, was definitely not your friend. He was the man whose chamber pot you emptied, whose breeches you scrubbed, whose gaze you avoided as you slipped through the dark hallways of his home.

You did your job and kept your head down. But you were in the wrong place at the wrong time when a great storm sent King James VI searching for someone to blame for his fright upon the high seas. Witches were the only answer, and your master was hungry for a witch hunt, hungry for favor from the zealot king.

A teenage girl is such a strange combination of powerful and powerless. Powerful in the perception of those who blame her for things like raising storms through witchcraft, in order to capsize a ship and kill a king and his new bride.

But with no power to defend against those accusations.

You were guilty before he ever asked a question and you weren't even in a court of law. There was no judge or jury, though executioner seemed imminent.

Only Master Seton and the men he wanted to impress, gathered in the room you'd scrubbed for their approval. The questions never ended.

Tell me of your dealings with the devil.
Where do you celebrate the devil's Sabbath?
Who else have you seen there?
How do you cast your spells?
Have you lain with the devil?
Do you understand this will go easier for you if you just tell the truth?

You were a sturdy girl. You'd have had to be to have survived this far at your station. But even you could not withstand a thrawing—the rope twisted and squeezed around your head. Even you were no match for thumbscrews.

Yes, you finally relented. I'm a witch.

You only wanted him to stop. You had no way to know your confession would inflame his witch-lust further. Not only his but his son's and their witch-hunting friends, all of whom wanted nothing more than power over someone else.

There's power in stripping off the clothes of a helpless girl and jeering at her to show her devil's mark. They'd seize upon anything—birthmark, bug bite, mole, scar. If only they'd looked in a glass, they could have seen devil's marks in their coal-black eyes, the grim slashes of hungry mouths across twisted faces.

But they focused only on you.

Shaking, pale, you couldn't show them what you didn't have. Rather than admit the lunacy of the request—in order to prove innocence, the accused must show an absence of something?—they doubled down, pinning you in place and shaving your body free of hair, searching for the impossible, the power they craved but that would never be sufficient.

While they had you there, a helpless girl naked and terrified, nothing stopped them from searching everywhere. In the name of righteousness, of course.

The only way to make it stop: *I do have a devil's mark!*

Triumphant in their victory over a little girl, they reported your confession to the king, who spun one terrified girl into an entire coven of madwomen intent on his destruction.

To demonstrate the might of the Scottish king to the rest of England, he wrote a pamphlet, *Newes from Scotland*, so the kingdom would know of his righteousness, his triumph over the cunning women who tried to capsize his ship but were vanquished instead.

Out of the muck-filled gutters of London, a young playwright picked up one of these trampled pamphlets and read of this gathering of witches deciding the fate of a king. He saw the drama, the possibility.

Fair is foul, and foul is fair. Hover through the fog and filthy air.

Now the whole world knows of those witches who brew toil and trouble in a cauldron upon a stage, but no one knows the name of Geillis Duncan.

You never had the chance to tell your story, Gilly. But I survived, and I'm not a child anymore. I'm telling your story and mine.

Geillis Duncan
(c 1577–1591, Scotland)
Geillis was a servant in the house of an ardent witch hunter. When King James VI's ship was turned back by a storm, he searched for someone to blame. Under extreme torture and likely rape, Geillis confessed to being part of a coven of witches who raised the storm.

Have I lain with the devil?
Lain so passive
as these men
asked children
if they'd had sex
with Satan.

Is it sex
if his sweet nothings
were bitter poison:

>how he found me
>repulsive, no one else could want
>me, believe me, redeem me,
>I made him do this
>he knew I wanted it
>no means yes
>means I didn't have a choice
>silly little girl
>little slut

I have.

Sophomore year of college
I have thrown myself
into my playwriting class.

It's all I talk about
when I speak to my parents.

Mark says this,
Mark says that.
There is no Advanced Playwriting
but Mark's going to mentor me
in an Independent Study.

In theater school
all professors are called
by their first names.

They don't all drive students home
after a late-night rehearsal
which might warrant a raised eyebrow

except that Mark
is fully uninterested in me
except as an exciting young playwright

and my fury
when my parents express concern
about the appropriateness
of my relationship with my (gay)
playwriting professor
is incandescent.

Now they're worried
about the time I'm spending
with an older man?

Conference Room #1

A girl I barely know
is going down the hall
in my dorm
searching for anyone

who wants to take the L
from our college suburb
into the heart of Chicago
to add a forty-hour training
and overnight volunteer shifts
on top of our course loads
to become sexual assault crisis counselors
for the YWCA of Metropolitan Chicago.

I took Intro to Women's Studies
at the end of freshman year, a whim,
my heart knowing what I needed before I did.
I have the most elementary of language
but I feel a pull to do this thing
so far outside my comfort zone
        (so close to my own experience).

We take the L from Evanston
down to the Loop
for the first session of our training
to staff hotlines, meet rape victims in ERs,
and teach community-center courses
about sexual assault and domestic violence.

We meet in a large conference room,
huge binders at each seat.
A passionate law student
leads the training.

I'm here on a whim, I tell myself,
but with every word, every statistic, every heartbreaking truth
I realize that's not why I'm here.
For the first time
I hear the definition of consent

and realize
a fifteen-year-old
a sixteen-year-old
a seventeen-year-old
cannot consent
to a grown man,
a church authority,
someone who's groomed her
with careful manipulation
to believe this is her choice, her fault,
                                      her sin.

I've thought of her
over the years,
the law student who gave me the language
to name what happened to me
and with that language
fight for justice
fight to protect others in my position.

I've thought about finding her
and telling her what that meant to me,
telling her how hard I've fought,
showing her the books I've written
with the language she gave me

because I want her to know
she is a link in this chain of stories
handed down from woman to woman
witch to witch
from Eve to Judith to Artemisia to me

each one taking a bite
before passing the apple along
the burst of knowledge sweet
upon each tongue.

I also think about her
because hers was the first baby
I ever stayed awake with
through a relentless night
unwilling to let a vulnerable creature
cry alone in darkness.

Some months after
the training at the YWCA
she got married
and asked me to care for her baby
during the ceremony and reception,
but also in a hotel room
through the whole wedding night.

I had babysitting experience
but I was a decade away
from having my own children,
from reading endless books
and consciously deciding

to ignore the experts who preach
that children should be trained to sleep
by leaving them alone, teaching them
that raising their voices has no effect.

Beginning on that first night
I spent with a baby
                    her baby

I knew instinctively I would never
teach a child I couldn't hear them
didn't care about
their pleas for help.

I track her down
and find out
we had more in common
than I knew at the time.

She had been studying opera in college
when she did the same YWCA training.
It diverted her course, too.

Instead of a life upon the stage
she became a lawyer
who worked on civil rights
and wrongful convictions.

That makes so much sense

        but then

        I see

                she has also
                defended

                      Bill Cosby

                        R. Kelly

                          Harvey Weinstein.

I'm losing my grip on reality.
I must be
        for there is no world
rooted in logic and consequence
where this outcome is possible.

How does a person go from
taking the YWCA rape crisis counselor
    training
and becoming a lawyer because of it,
later teaching the training herself

to not only defending
some of the most egregious serial predators
but attacking their victims on the stand,
accusing them of being liars, racists,
    extortionists?

That's how journalists describe
her style of defense: aggressive.

I can't understand.
It's a record scratch
on the story I've told
for years.

I call my editor.
I text close friends.
Everyone is baffled.

Capitalism, someone suggests
as an explanation, and perhaps
but there are lesser devils
bidding on souls.

She could have become
an oil lobbyist
or a social media oligarch
or even a lawyer defending murderers
out of the conviction
that everyone deserves a defense.

> *I'm supposed to be*
> *some type of ambassador1*
> *—a vagina ambassador,*

>> she told a reporter.

> *Seriously, I get a lot of*
> *those questions,*
> *like somehow I am*
> *traitorous to women*
> *by taking on these cases.*

She sneers at the maxim

> *believe women*

meanwhile
she has a tattoo
that says

> *not guilty*

and isn't that just the flip side
of believing all women, always?
Declaring the defendant is never guilty?

If the devotion were to the process
then the tattoo would read

> *presumed innocent.*

I don't know how
to process this discovery
that's come so late in the
making of this book—

> it has a cover and an ISBN,
> sales and marketing people
> are already previewing
> a draft without this piece
> of my story

I simply don't have the time
to grapple with this

as though with any amount of time
there will be a way
to make sense of this.

But I can't leave it out either.

I can't give you the children's Bible version
reducing it to a smiling white lady
with fig leaves covering her offensive parts,
eating an apple from a cartoon snake

when the truth is
soon she will be violently cast out
of the only home she's ever known
into a wilderness
of predators around every corner

and the only person she'll have
at her side
is the man who told God
it was all her fault.

I've eaten the fruit of knowledge
and I'm beginning to understand
my teenage years.

It should be freeing
but instead
I'm ashamed,
want to cover
my nakedness.

I'm back in it
panicked
gutted
horrified
undone

even though
I'm states away
it's over now
it wasn't a man with a gun.

I sit immobile
in my college apartment
staring at the poster on my wall
of Marilyn Monroe
      subject of my first play
trying to hold up
a falling-down costume
never meant to contain her,
her eyes my only anchor.

How do you find your way back in the dark?

The first line of that play
written this same year
that I put language to my pain,
spoken by Marilyn

        the last line
        she ever spoke on-screen.

Cowards, my Marilyn says.
You are all cowards and opportunists
and small, sick bastards
who'll stick your hands
up a little girl's dress
to get what you want.

I start to cut myself
on my thighs
and upper arms
with a kitchen knife
I keep in my room
for this purpose.

Over the college years
I have started
to be kinder to my body
nourishing it, allowing a hint of curve
but now I am a raw nerve

a gaping wound
I can't comprehend
since I'm safe
he'll never touch me again
he'll never control me

but if I slice open my flesh
I can see the blood
and make sense
of the excruciating pain.

It's not a suicidal thing,
I write in an email to a friend
who is concerned by my self-harm.

It's a need for tangible pain
an affirmation
that if I can bleed
I must still be alive

a feeling that
if anyone is going to hurt my body
it's going to be me.

I'm sure none of that makes sense.
It's the best I can do.

Dear Marion,

As I tumble down this putrid hole of women accused, coerced, convicted, executed, I find a spot of light: your story of strength, conviction, the astounding courage to stand up against men who would have burned you if they hadn't been too busy defending themselves against your truth.

You could have stayed silent. No one named you as a witch.

But you saw the madness unfolding as an accused woman saved herself by claiming she could look into people's eyes and divine their guilt or innocence. The Great Witch of Balwearie was dragged all over the land to perform her trick and condemn countless women to death in her stead.

Did you pity her? Or did you admire her instinct for survival? Did you wonder how she could go from the terror of being accused to turning that terror on other women?

Either way, you could have kept your thoughts to yourself. Most people did, cowering in fragile security.

But something compelled you to speak, to action. Had they burnt someone you loved? Had the Great Witch of Balwearie looked into the eyes of your friends, your sisters, and declared them the devil's handmaidens?

Or had you simply had enough of men like Reverend John Cowper, who declared themselves the voice of God despite shriveled souls and cruel hearts, so far from the God you worshipped?

The Great Witch was found fraudulent, declaring the same woman both guilty and innocent after she'd done nothing more than change her clothes. She sent hundreds of women to their deaths, in order to prove her own innocence. Surely it would have been proven after only a few. Was she forced to keep staring into the eyes of strangers and deciding their fates? Or did she get caught up in the power, the security of being on the side with the torches?

Once the Great Witch was exposed, did you know that the men who'd been pulling her strings would then cover up the fraud, rather than let the truth come out? Did you think, *Of course they'll bury it. That's what the church always does.*

But the people deserved to know their wives, mothers, sisters, friends had not been witches. For they believed, even if you did not, that the devil could steal the souls of the wicked and drag them down to hell.

They deserved to know the Great Witch of Balwearie saw nothing but veins when she examined the rivers of red crisscrossing the eyes of the accused and claimed she could read their souls.

But mostly they deserved to know that the church they'd put their faith in, the church they gave power and tithes to, had slaughtered their loved ones based on a fraud and even worse, they'd covered up the truth.

No one else was going to tell this truth, so you did. You spoke up, spread the truth across the city, throughout the countryside. You were respected, no madwoman or accused witch broken down into forced confessions in the hope of an end to their torture. You weren't a king trying to shore up power by proving how very close to God you were.

You were simply a woman willing to speak the truth.

You must have been afraid. Terrified. But instead of letting that fear conquer you, you conquered it.

You told the truth, passed it hand to hand, even when the Presbytery threatened torture for anyone who blamed them for witchcraft executions.

(Why don't women come forward?)

Denounced, berated, belittled, threatened, you never wavered.

Finally the power-hungry king called off his hunt. And somehow you were lost to history.

Whether or not we know your name (I know your name), we descendants of the women who didn't burn owe you our lives, our voices.

Thank you, Marion.

I'll never stop using my voice.

Marion Walker
(c 1597–c 1657, Scotland)
Marion discovered not only the church's fraud in using the Great Witch of Balwearie to identify other witches, but also their cover-up of the fraud. She spread the word, despite the threat of torture for anyone who blamed the Presbytery for witchcraft executions.

To the angry girl

That lump of coal
stuck in your throat
is not meant to be expelled
but refined.

It's a part of you
skin teeth fury
they'd reach down your throat
to wrench it out
because they know
its worth.

They know
if you keep it, cherish it
scrape off the rough edges
you'll be left with a glittering gem

that can cut through any lies.

A child gains language
a word at a time,
devoted parents hovering,
cheering every new sound
that drops from milky lips.

I'm a college student
excelling at language
but suddenly
words have new meanings
memories shift, whole relationships
built on the San Andreas Fault
have suddenly ruptured.

If I couldn't consent
if I wasn't to blame
if I was coerced

if he could do that to me
then he could do it to anyone
could be doing it to another girl
this very second.

When the woman who taught me
that a sixteen-year-old cannot consent
to a grown man
cross-examines one of Bill Cosby's victims,
she'll challenge her on why
it took her so long to come forward.1

Sixteen years old in 1975,
Judy Huth met a film star in a park.
He invited her and a friend
to the Playboy Mansion
where he sexually assaulted her
and she couldn't leave
because she hadn't driven herself
so she stayed for several more hours

and the defense attorney said—
the woman who taught me how trauma responses
    vary—said,

    Boy, did Judy and Donna enjoy themselves.

Victims come forward in their own time
as they have the language,
the resources,
the more fully developed brains
to comprehend power dynamics,
to understand rape isn't only
the stranger in the alley with the gun,
to realize the shame isn't theirs.

Some never come forward.

When I had the language

when I understood the stakes
when I realized this was a pattern
and there would be other girls,
I came forward immediately

but I'll never stop wondering
if things might have turned out differently
if I'd known to come forward sooner.

I am still grateful
to that young law student.

I can't disentangle her
from my story

even though she has shown me
what a woman *can* do.

If I hadn't done that training
or someone else had taught it

I would have eventually
gained that knowledge

but the fact is
I gained it then, from her

and that set in motion
each next step of the story

>which detectives handled my case

>who was in leadership at the church

>even my decision to graduate early
>and move to Guatemala
>where I met my husband.

I want to say
she didn't give me the language.
I took it for myself.

I do say that, in a previous draft,
in a poem my editor says
isn't quite landing.

He's right, it's not.
Because it's not true.
At least not completely.

She literally did
teach me the meaning
of those life-altering words:

      consent, abuse, sexual assault, rape

and helped me see
how they fit
into the context of my own life.

Just like my father instilled in me
a love of reading and story,
a desire to express myself in writing.

I can be grateful to them both
for what they gave me
while despising the choices they made.

      Brett, on the other hand,
      gave me nothing
      but gaping wounds.

He has to be stopped.
But it isn't straightforward.
Neither Brett nor my dad
works at that church
any longer.

My dad is now
president of a seminary.
Brett is shaping young souls
at a different San Diego church.

I need someone
who will know what to do.

Conference Room #2

For spring break, I visit April
at school in Colorado
where Tom now lives,
the youth pastor
who moved away
in the middle of my freshman year.
Longtime family friend,
the youth pastor I should have had,
the one who will know what to do.

I've told him I'm coming,
I need to talk.
He shows me around his new digs,
a video production company,
and at the end of the tour
we sit down in another conference room.

So Joy. Why are we here?

Tom listens well.
He's returned to San Diego
over the years, interviewed me
for topical videos he makes
for youth leaders—body image, eating disorders.
He's coached me to speak in first person,
instead of hiding behind third.

    The difference between saying

        You feel more in control
        when you decide what you eat

  and

        I feel more in control
        when I decide what I eat.

He's nodded thoughtfully
many times before and said,

    Say more about that

and it has always been genuine
but it has never been like this.

    You do understand
    that I'm a mandated reporter?

I do.
That's why I've come.

A mandated reporter
is someone who is legally obligated to report suspected child abuse or neglect to authorities.

According to California Penal Code a mandated reporter is defined as any of the following:

(1) A teacher.
(2) An instructional aide.
(3) A teacher's aide or teacher's assistant employed by a public or private school.
(4) A classified employee of a public school.
(5) An administrative officer or supervisor of child welfare and attendance, or a certificated pupil personnel employee of a public or private school.
(6) An administrator of a public or private day camp.
(7) An administrator or employee of a public or private youth center, youth recreation program, or youth organization.
(8) An administrator, board member, or employee of a public or private organization whose duties require direct contact and supervision of children, including a foster family agency.
(9) An employee of a county office of education or the State Department of Education whose duties bring the employee into contact with children on a regular basis.
(10) A licensee, an administrator, or an employee of a licensed community care or child daycare facility.
(11) A Head Start program teacher.
(12) A licensing worker or licensing evaluator employed by a licensing agency.
(13) A public assistance worker.
(14) An employee of a childcare institution, including, but not limited to, foster parents, group home personnel, and personnel of residential care facilities.
(15) A social worker, probation officer, or parole officer.
(16) An employee of a school district police or security department.
(17) A person who is an administrator or presenter of, or a counselor in, a child abuse prevention program in a public or private school.
(18) A district attorney investigator, inspector, or local child support agency caseworker.
(19) A peace officer.
(20) A firefighter.
(21) A physician and surgeon, psychiatrist, psychologist, dentist, resident, intern, podiatrist, chiropractor, licensed nurse, dental hygienist, optometrist, marriage and family therapist, clinical social worker, professional clinical counselor, or any other person who is currently licensed.
(22) An emergency medical technician I or II, or paramedic.
(23) A psychological assistant.
(24) A marriage and family therapist trainee.
(25) An unlicensed associate marriage and family therapist.

(26) A state or county public health employee who treats a minor for venereal disease or any other condition.
(27) A coroner.
(28) A medical examiner or other person who performs autopsies.
(29) A commercial film and photographic print or image processor.
(30) A child visitation monitor.
(31) An animal control officer or humane society officer.
(32) A clergy member. As used in this article, "clergy member" means a priest, minister, rabbi, religious practitioner, or similar functionary of a church, temple, or recognized denomination or organization.
(33) Any custodian of records of a clergy member.
(34) An employee of any police department, county sheriff's department, county probation department, or county welfare department.
(35) An employee or volunteer of a Court Appointed Special Advocate program.
(36) A custodial officer.
(37) A person providing Welfare services to a minor child.
(38) An alcohol and drug counselor for a state licensed or certified drug, alcohol, or drug and alcohol treatment program.
(39) A clinical counselor trainee.
(40) An associate professional clinical counselor.
(41) An employee or administrator of a public or private postsecondary educational institution, whose duties bring the administrator or employee into contact with children on a regular basis, or who supervises those whose duties bring the administrator or employee into contact with children on a regular basis, as to child abuse or neglect occurring on that institution's premises or at an official activity of, or program conducted by, the institution.
(42) An athletic coach, athletic administrator, or athletic director employed by any public or private school that provides any combination of instruction for kindergarten, or grades 1 to 12, inclusive.
(43) (A)   A commercial computer technician who works for a company that is in the business of repairing, installing, or otherwise servicing a computer or computer component, including, but not limited to, a computer part, device, memory storage or recording mechanism, auxiliary storage recording or memory capacity, or any other material relating to the operation and maintenance of a computer or computer network system, for a fee.
(44) Any athletic coach, including, but not limited to, an assistant coach or a graduate assistant involved in coaching, at public or private postsecondary educational institutions.
(45) An individual certified by a licensed foster family agency as a certified family home.
(46) An individual approved as a Welfare and Institutions resource family.
(47) A qualified autism service provider, a qualified autism service professional, or a qualified autism service paraprofessional.
(48) A human resource employee of a business subject to Part 2.8 (commencing with Section 12900) of Division 3 of Title 2 of the Government Code that employs minors.
(49) An adult person whose duties require direct contact with and supervision of minors in the performance of the minors' duties in the workplace of a business.

Bringing charges forward
means telling the church
and the police

but it also means
telling my parents
my sister
my friends
whose entire high school experiences
were centered on this man.

I know
I am doing the right thing
but I also know
I am about to hurt
so
many
people.

Phone Call #1

I call my sister
who's gone as far away as possible,
living in Australia
while her husband
attends seminary.

*I need to tell you
that when I was in high school
Brett sexually abused me.*

> (*Abuse* the word
> I'm trying out,
> on my way to naming it
> as rape.)

She's quiet. Too quiet
even for the sister
who's always been reserved.
Finally she speaks,
her voice strangled.

> *Joy, I have to go.*

Of all the responses I'd imagined
hanging up on me was not one of them.
She calls me back a few hours later.

> *I have to tell you . . .*
> *He did the same thing to me.*

I watched from the window
as my sister climbed into Brett's truck
and I was jealous,
thought I wanted what she had.

I got it.

She was only in San Diego
for one semester
before leaving for college,
and the moment she did,
he turned his sights on me.
Monstrous, but not even the worst part
of what she tells me.

My distraught sister,
before she left for Chicago,
guilt-ridden and blaming herself
but thinking of me and others
went to my father, the senior pastor,
and told him what Brett had done to her.

Too ashamed to tell him everything,
she held back, and even claimed
it had been her fault. But
she told him enough
that a mandated reporter
would be compelled to action.

Instead of legal action
or even firing Brett, my father
gave him grace—the same grace
he preached constantly from the pulpit.

Shouldn't we at least tell Joy? my sister asked.

*No. We don't want to ruin her
youth group experience.*

A mandated reporter
is someone who is legally obligated
to report suspected child abuse or neglect
to authorities.

According to California Penal Code
a mandated reporter is defined as
any of the following:

(32) A clergy member. As used in this article, "clergy member" means a priest, minister, rabbi, religious practitioner, or similar functionary of a church, temple, or recognized denomination or organization.

Phone Call #2

I call my father.
He's quiet
but a different kind of quiet
from Tom listening thoughtfully

or my sister panicking
at the bomb I've dropped
into her world.

He's waiting me out.
When I've finished and told him
I'm pressing charges, he says,

> *Are you sure that's a good idea?*
> *You need to think very carefully.*

You need to think very carefully.

As though
any part of the muck
we're both drowning in
is because I have not thought about this

although *think* may not be the word
for how my body yanks me back
to the guilt, the vigilance, the confusion, the fear

the way I fight sleep
mind racing
and when I finally succumb
my dreams yank me back to the same place again

        how it took me years
        to come forward
        years that mean
        no charges will be pressed
        for lack of physical evidence

        and it wasn't
        that I was just going about my life
        through those years
        before suddenly deciding
        without thought
        to do this thing
        that will bring my life
        tumbling down
        around me.

        Imagine how many pelicans
        I could have pondered

in all the time I have spent
thinking
about
this.

Pelicans
feature prominently
in my dad's memoir
that covers this same period of time

which is out of print
but the resourceful reader
     like my editor
can find it.

   He doesn't mention
   what happened to you
   or your sister.

I'm honestly baffled
by the idea that he would.

I think he would say
it's not his story to tell.

   He presents
   the great tragedy of his life
   as losing his job
   without even a hint
   of something far worse
   happening in his family.

I sit with this.
It's jarring
when someone looks in
on a family from the outside
through a window cut into a door
by my words, my father's words
and names everything that's broken
with perfect clarity.

No, but the thing is
he doesn't think
he did anything wrong
in handling Brett—

He doesn't have to!
Even if he were blameless
the great tragedy
in your family
was not him losing his job!
It's as though I got in an accident
in which my right elbow got bruised
and my left leg was completely
    severed,
but in writing about the accident
I only talk about my elbow
and allow you to believe
I had no other injuries.

My editor's vehement indignation
belongs to a parent
who would be utterly broken
if something similar
happened to his children

who would give up
his remaining limbs
if he could do anything to save them
from bleeding out
on the sidewalk.

For context:

My father didn't lose his job
for any reason related to
mishandling Brett.

He lost his job and
his ordination as a Presbyterian minister

        which he got back
        a few years later

for affairs with a church secretary
and an associate pastor
which the governing body
of the Presbyterian church
deemed sexual abuse.

Phone Call #3 (I think?)

I don't remember
calling my mother.
I must have.
My parents had divorced by then.
She would have cried.

Dear Christian,

I have to be honest. Your story doesn't unfold the way I'd like it to. The conclusions aren't forgone. Each time I approach it, I see it from another angle. But I won't set it aside in favor of one of the other thousands of stories that could fill these pages. That's not fair to you. Many of these stories are complex and nuanced and don't fit into neat categories.

They still matter.

And what's more—what's the most important to me, in fact—you were a child. You had no agency. Even if I view your story through the worst possible lens, you weren't a grown woman with choices and options, hands sticky from the fruit of knowledge.

No, your hands smarted from the switches you'd received for sneaking a biscuit meant for guests.

Stealing is sinful, your father had told you.

So when you found the maid drinking from a bottle of milk belonging to your family, you told her, *That's not yours.*

For there should be justice in the world, shouldn't there?

But she scoffed at you, underestimated you, and that wouldn't stand.

I'll tell my father you're a thief.

For a moment it seemed the maid would hang her head, repent, remember her place, and you would have done some good in the world. But perhaps that day her place had been too much to bear and you were only a powerless child, so she unloaded on you what she longed to say to the laird and his wife:

I wish the devil would haul your soul through hell.

You weren't powerless.

You would make her wish come true, dragging her right along behind you. You knew what hell was like, what witches could do. You listened in church, you learned your lessons. You lingered in doorways to scandalized voices discussing accusations, blasphemies, and punishments. You'd bring hell to Bargarran and no one would ever underestimate you again.

It was simple.

You'd heard salacious details of the girls across the ocean who'd brought an entire town to its knees in prayer and pleading for their lives. Abigail Williams had been just your age when she accused Elizabeth Proctor. People underestimated her too. They paid for it.

Convulsions are easy to fake. The stabbing pains, night terrors, body gone rigid, eyes rolled back, spouting scripture. Playing pretend.

What required more commitment were the wads of hair and coal and eggshells you spit up, especially when you couldn't simply slip them into your mouth, but had to swallow them down and force them back up. But by that point you were in too deep (*only a witch would float*) and there was no going back.

No matter how it started, you were truly tormented now.

Except I'm not sure this version rings true: a girl so enraged by a housemaid's simple theft that she scorched the earth her town stood upon. That sounds to me like a story written by the people in power, who didn't want to take responsibility—judges and magistrates and witnesses and executioners who actually carried it all out.

Perhaps it had nothing to do with the maid. Perhaps you simply fell ill. And to your parents' credit, they didn't leap directly to witches. They took you to the family doctor and the local apothecary, who did their best. But bloodletting has never yet solved an illness of the brain.

They swept you off to the big city of Glasgow, where more learned doctors, specialists, apothecaries applied endless tests and treatments. The trouble was, there was no name then for encephalitis, epilepsy, pica. Whatever truly ailed you, they were never going to find it.

There was only one way to stop the endless tests, poking, prodding, bleeding:

I was bewitched!

But I think it was likely more complex than those two options: evil or ill. You would have been told of sins and damnation and the age of accountability for years. The devil had been more insistent on your mind than the savior since the first brimstone sermon you understood as a toddler squirming on unforgiving pews. You were all too aware that soon you would be twelve, soon your wicked actions would have eternal consequences.

Of course the devil consumed your thoughts. How could anyone go about their day ignoring the peril in every step? With one wrong move, one sharp word, one impure thought, one mistake, the devil would have a foothold in your soul.

(Do you know, *Don't give the devil a foothold* would be an endless youth group refrain centuries later?)

If grown and pious men had succumbed to the devil, how were you, an eleven-year-old girl, to stand a chance? The maid had cursed you, yes. But you'd been greedy and uncharitable first. You threatened her.

Perhaps the devil already had his foothold in your soul.

You had to show how pure you were, how righteous. Show your parents and the brimstone preacher. Show yourself. What would a pure girl do?

Expel the devil.

Each time you cried out in pain, convulsed, went mute, you showed your strength.

Look how she resists the devil!

Each time you quoted scriptures you'd heard a million times, you showed your piety. Each time you named a witch, you had everyone's attention and maybe you convinced yourself you'd done enough to save your soul.

Whatever the truth of your story, centuries later the few who learn your name will know you vomited coal. But they'll miss the footnote about what came later.

You traveled to Holland, smuggled back designs and equipment to introduce Scotland to fine silk and linen thread. You advised the Board of Trade. You opened spinning schools. Your Bargarran Thread Company would fade from the history books, but the techniques you brought to Scotland would lead directly to the Coats and Clark thread I use today.

So many of the women in these pages died too early—either hung or burnt or crushed by the weight of childhood actions. You survived. You thrived.

As I stitch these stories together, I'm so focused on crafting the polished piece of work everyone will see, but turn it over and there's a chaos of tangled threads, the messy places where different colors cross one another, where some threads are snipped away, where the snarled knots secure the beauty of the other side.

There's truth and art in both.

Christian Shaw
(1685–1737, Scotland)
Christian was an eleven-year-old girl who accused thirty-five people of witchcraft, six of whom were executed and one died by suicide. Her symptoms of possession were extreme: vomiting coal, balls of hair, and chicken feathers; convulsing and ranting scripture. She later went on to revolutionize the Scottish thread industry.

Conference Room #3

I fly to San Diego next,
the palm trees and sea air
inducing panic
as soon as I leave the airport.

Tom's arranged
for Ken, a family friend and lawyer
to accompany me to my interview
with the sex crimes division
of the San Diego Police Department.

I'd prefer Tom
but he'll come later
for the conversations with churches.
War veteran Ken is an attack dog
who loves me and is ready for battle
as we walk into the police station together.
It turns out, his fury isn't required.

The detectives who speak to me
are compassionate.
A man and a woman, they hear
my story, ask specific questions
that stick with me.

How many fingers did he insert?

Does it matter?
Do the charges change
if it's one finger
or two, or three?
        (It was three.)

They write everything down,
treat me with respect.

For a few years after
every time I hear horror stories
of police misconduct around sexual assault
I'll think, *I was so lucky
my case was handled well.*

Until I find out
that after my case was moved
to another jurisdiction

an officer there
had a daughter in the youth group
a close friend of Brett's
who everyone called "Brett's new Joy"
after I moved away.

      In 2015 my friend Krista
      is grappling with her own experience
      of youth group and how it was reshaped
          later
      by learning what had happened to me.

      She begins reaching out to people
      to understand their perspectives.
      She still attends the church
      and doesn't want the history forgotten.

      She remembers the girl known as
      "Brett's new Joy"
      and reaches out to her.
      The girl—woman now—is furious.
      She is still close to Brett.

      She tells Krista her father
      let her read my case file
      and that's how she knows
      my story was

              inconsistent, full of lies

and there's no way to know
if her claim is true
but if it is
what a massive breach of ethics

and the one part of my story
that felt redemptive

my cautious faith
that the justice system
had done its best for me

        shattered to pieces.

As I excavate history
to write this book
I locate the detective
who championed my case.

>*I remember this case very well.*1
>*I was a young detective*
>*and rather zealous at solving the case*
>*in the name of justice.*
>
>*But I was shut down*
>*by a higher-ranking officer*
>*in my venture for the victim.*
>
>*I was angry at this order given.*
>*He wasn't even from my command*
>*but I obeyed the order.*
>
>*Please accept my sincerest apologies.*

I tell him on a phone call
how grateful I am
for how he made me feel at the time
that he believed me.

His next words mean more to me
than he will ever know.

>*You know what?*
>*I still do.*

Dear Katherine,

Sitting in the kitchen after the rest of the household had gone to sleep, you regaled your fellow servants with stories. You took a maid's hand and examined the lines on her palm. You tried to remember the words in a book you'd read before you sailed across the seas to begin a life in the New World, a book by a man who hailed from humble beginnings like yours and made his name and fortune reading stars.

If he could do it, why not you?

You furrowed your brow, adopted a thoughtful expression, then told her what she wanted to hear about the stable boy.

Katherine can see the future! she told the others.

Always stargazing, you managed to marry beyond your station. Not astronomically but enough that when your landowning husband died you became a woman of means. You wanted the same for your daughters, petitioning the court to apportion them part of the estate. The first of many times the courts would ignore you.

Until this point you'd never had trouble with neighbors or the law. You'd never been accused of anything untoward. But now you were a woman with property of your own and no man to control you. You had to be stopped.

After all, you should have seen it coming. In the stars, in your palms, in the world opposing you at every turn.

Your neighbors were reasonable people. They didn't start with witchcraft. Instead they brutally attacked your livestock, wounding and killing oxen, pigs, cattle. So strange the sudden calamities that befell the farm—crops trampled, vandalism—once there was no longer a man in charge. Perhaps the widow didn't have the stomach for such a business. Perhaps she should marry, or leave Wethersfield entirely.

Back when you first learned to read the stars, you saw a different kind of life, a meteoric rise. And you'd been right so far—from servant girl to widow so wealthy the town rose up against her.

You saw no reason to back down. You didn't need a husband, but you'd follow the rest of their rules. You petitioned the courts, lodged complaints, worked within a justice system that had no place for you.

(So did I.)

There was no response.

When the court finally listened, it wasn't to you. It was to the town, who'd tired of sabotaging the farm—a bit messy, that. Easier to call you a witch.

The accusations flew as fast as a witch on her way to kiss the devil's ass at Sabbath.

Some of the charges against you:

spinning yarn too well

predicting the future and occasionally being right

lying

breaking the (Lord's) Sabbath

milking a cow not your own

hovering near a sick person.

No one could claim you'd harmed a soul but thirty-eight men petitioned against you and a jury found you guilty. After two years of court proceedings, you were to hang.

You didn't, though. You weren't wrong all those years ago when you envisioned a life that blazed brighter than those around you.

Your execution was stayed as the court consulted with clergy. Somehow, as though it had been written in the stars, the verdict was overturned. But you were banished from the colony; you paid your court fees and fled.

Some systems are too entrenched, institutions immovable. I know it too well. But I still see your star, Katherine, blazing across the sky.

Katherine Harrison
(c 1625–c 1682, Wethersfield, CT)
Katherine was a servant who dabbled in fortune-telling and married above her station. She became a landowner and her neighbors vandalized her farm; when that didn't run her out of town, they turned to witchcraft accusations.

Conference Room #4

The church has prospered and grown,
moved into new offices
since I went away to college,
since my father left to head a seminary,
since Brett moved on
to a new church
with a clean slate—

                and I have to be so careful
                about what I say next
                about anything that came after
                Brett moved out of my immediate orbit
                anything I didn't witness
                with my own eyes

                because he still holds the power
                over how I tell this story
                he still looms as a threat
                if I dare to tell
                my story

                one second past
                the last time I saw him

                          which was on a down escalator
                          at a movie theater
                          as I was going up
                          a few months after
                          I first told the police
                          my story

                but the thing is
                my story

isn't only
what he did to me.

Whatever he did next
after me
is part of my story
because I have lived for decades
with the fear, the festering wound,
the oppressive anxiety

        I race from the escalator
        burst out of the movie theater
        and curl myself over a railing
        bile in my throat

that my failure to act soon enough

        if I'd had the guts
                to leave Brett standing
                there
        guts churning, turning

left him free
to strike again.

But I can't say anything
about what he did next.
I can't even imply it.

I can say this, though:

As women we're required
to couch and qualify our language
to make ourselves small
so as not to possibly offend anyone

and it's infuriating
when we've excised that conditioning
and learned to own our entire stories
without apology
to be asked to couch it again
in order to comply with the system
built to protect the men
who made us small
to begin with.

Do I know for a fact
that's provable in a court of law
that there are victims willing to come forward
other pastors' daughters
or indeed any additional victims
after me?

No.
That's the fact, for the lawyers.

Do I know from decades
of living with trauma
learning about shame and predators
about power dynamics and serial abusers,
decades of being a woman in this fucking world

that a man does not prey on three teenage girls
all pastors' daughters he has authority over
with eerily similar sexual, emotional, and spiritual
 abuse
and then stop
and never abuse again?

Yes.

I know it
in my silly, estrogen-addled heart,
in my delicate lady bones,
to the deepest fibers of my frail, feminine being.

But don't pay me any mind.
I must be on the rag.

Conference Room #4, Redux

The church has prospered and grown,
moved into new offices
since I went away to college,
since my father left to head a seminary,
since Brett moved on to a different church.

It's a blessing, I think,
for surely the old, familiar offices
would flood me with memories
drown me in ordeal by water
but also it's a bandage
on a gaping, festering wound.

My racing heart
knows exactly
where I am.

I meet the pastor
who has succeeded my father
in a conference room
with other church leaders,
some of whom have known me
since I learned to read the Bible.

They know why I'm here.
But still my own voice
must be strong enough to say it.

Dear Bridget,

When I read the transcript of your trial, I felt the same connection I felt in reading the transcript of Artemisia's trial. We stand before the men in power and speak our truths even as they crush our joints.

> *I am innocent.*

> *Why do you seem to act witchcraft before us?*

> *I know nothing of it.*
> *I am innocent to a witch.*
> *I know not what a witch is.*

> *How do you know then that you are not a witch?*

> *I do not know what you say.*

> *How can you know you are no witch,*
> *and yet not know what a witch is?*

> *I am clear:*
> *if I were any such person*
> *you should know it.*

> *You may threaten, but you can do no more*
> *than you are permitted.*

> *I am innocent of a witch.*

You were innocent of a witch, but not of the way men could twist things, like the husband who beat you, then left you bruised in the town square, pilloried for raising your voice against him, spread open to the gossip and the lies, the examination of your body for your fault.

You were no stranger to injustices of the courts, since that husband who beat you bloody escaped the stocks when his daughter paid his fines but they left you there.

His final blow: leaving you the land his children would destroy you for, accusing you of witchcraft to cheat you out of what you'd earned for surviving him. Did he foresee the headaches that land would bring you?

You weren't the first to be accused of witchcraft, but you were the first tried in the courts of Salem. Not because your case was so egregious, but because the authorities (men) like a case they can win.

You were a thrice-married woman who'd already been in trouble with the law. Of course they could win, and you would be the first to hang for the crime of witchcraft in Salem, the New World, land of possibility

As the first to die in Salem, you should be remembered. But still you're mixed up with Sarah Bishop, accused for running a tavern and wearing a red corset.

(*What was she wearing?*)

Does it change anything that your accusers retracted their claims after you were dead? And yet the government never cleared your name.

Here's what I'll remember of you, Bridget:

> *I am clear:*
> *if I were any such person*
> *you should know it.*

Truly. If we were anywhere near as powerful as they want to claim we are, would we still be standing before them, begging for our lives?

Bridget Bishop
(c 1632–1692, Salem, MA)
Bridget was the first person executed for witchcraft in Salem. She was married three times, and had been punished in the stocks for arguing with an abusive husband in public.

To the girl who tells her truth

Just because you tell it
doesn't mean anyone will listen
or if they listen, they might not believe

but it still matters
that you said it,
that you believe it

that you show them
who you are
and that you're not
afraid to speak.

To the girl who keeps her truth
safe in her heart,
I know you have good reason,
you probably know speaking up
would be more dangerous
than staying quiet.

It doesn't make you less
of a warrior, a survivor.
You've had to be so strong
with no one to help you carry the weight

but even if you never say the words,
I hear them. I believe you.
It wasn't your fault.

Brett denies everything
when detectives question him.
Of course he does.

He gets away with it
like most abusers
who don't even get accused

                                              but I like to think
                                              that he had at least
                                              a moment's terror
                                              when detectives came knocking.
                                              Maybe this time
                                              he wouldn't slip
                                              through their grasp
                                              so easily.

                                              But that's a fantasy
                                              because the truth is
                                              he was such a good liar

he's convinced even himself
he never did a single thing I said.

I'm crazy.

Crazy
means she can't be trusted
means lies fall from her lips
false as those Salem girls
convulsing for show

means when she comes around
telling her sob stories
you don't have to listen
don't give it a second thought
send her on her way

never knowing (or maybe you do)
that you're taking something from her
all over again, every time
you hear her words and take his side.

Which is worse?

Stories of clergy
who abuse their power,
confess, repent, receive forgiveness,
then do it all over again
like a liturgy repeated
until it's lost all meaning

or

to be denied that farce
and never have it acknowledged at all
without even a chance
for a church to say

> *We know this happened
> but we just don't care.*

The churches he moves to next
don't care
when I contact them
with my story
and offer witnesses.

One pastor
says when warned:

> *Girls these days*
> *will say anything.*

Another deigns
to speak with me by phone.

> *Why did you wait so long to come forward?*

He promises there'll be a thorough investigation.
My letter gives him contact information for

> two therapists
> the junior high youth pastor
> April and Tom
> and a family friend
> > a respected theologian
> > who will vouch for me.

He never contacts any of them.

I write a poem
and mail it
to his current church.
I'm not a poet.

I've never tried
the form before.

                        But even then
                        I knew instinctually
                        this is the only way
                        I can tell these stories.

It's not a good poem.
But it's real.

1-17-01

Blood

You made me bleed.
Or have the clouds of self-involved delusion so
    obscured your view
that you no longer see?
If that's the case,
I'll gladly paint the picture that forever haunts my
    mind.
One young girl with nothing to hold on to,
laid out, terrified, gazing at the ceiling while a
    monster takes away
the precious part of her that never was again.
Do you remember now?

Once he knows
I won't be silenced,
Brett gets ahead of my story
                (the truth).

With each new church
he moves to
I imagine
he brings me up
at the start.

> *Just so you know*
> *there's this troubled young woman*
> *obsessed with me, it's really sad.*
> *Mentally unstable, eating disorder,*
> *difficult home life.*
> *She has wild stories,*
> *but the police never brought charges.*
> *There was no evidence, you see.*

That's the thing about how long it takes
to process trauma and tell a story.
When years have gone by, there are no more
DNA samples to be found.
He didn't leave a written record.
So many people knew things were off
but no one knows anything for sure.

When my sister decides
she's willing to go on the record
the detective tells me
she can't corroborate my story
since we're sisters
and could have conspired together

and in fact
that because our stories are so similar
it seems obvious
we have conspired

                                          never mind the fact
                                          that even as of this writing
                                          we have never
                                          told each other
                                          our stories directly.

When I read my dad's memoir
all these years later
I realize
Brett was not the only storyteller
shouting down my story
in favor of his own.

Nobel Peace Prize winner
Archbishop Desmond Tutu
called my dad's book
        which completely erases
           his complicity in my horrors
"searingly honest"

and Presbyterian luminary
Frederick Buechner
        whose memoir *Telling Secrets*
           gave me courage as I told my own
called my dad's book
"honest and unsparing."

Lauded men of the cloth
will always have
a louder voice than mine.

The same church
harbored Brett
for many years.
I told them early on
who he is.
They didn't listen.

When I wrote a book
that won awards
about the rape of an artist
by her mentor
I thought about sending it to his church.

> *For the young women*
> *in your youth group,*
> *I'd inscribe it.*

When I wrote a book
about a rapist-hunting lady knight
I thought about sending it to his church.

> *For the young women*
> *who've survived your youth group,*
> *I'd inscribe it.*

As I write this book
I think about sending it
as an ember to set his world ablaze.

> *Would I really endure*
> *the massive undertaking*
> *of fabricating an entire memoir*
> *enduring the legal scrutiny*
> *risking a backlash*

*just for the heartbreak of being told
you still don't believe me?*

*Or worse
that you believe me
and still don't care?*

Wading through the paper trail
shared with me
by people who've stood by my side
and had the foresight
to hold on to this story

it baffles me
that the case against Brett
never moved forward,
that no one has stopped him
from working with youth.

And then I'm put in touch
with a specialist in church sexual abuse
brought in by the church where I grew up
to help change the culture of secrecy and lies,
abuse of power, which wasn't limited
to Brett and my dad.

She's an expert with no personal stake
no reason to lie
and her notes
tell me a new
and alarming detail:

> *the most painful was [the senior pastor's] decision to keep a charismatic youth minister on staff even after his daughters complained about being molested by him. No complaints were taken to the sheriff and when one daughter went to the [authorities] herself her father said she was a troubled child and spoke against her.*

I go into physical shock
on reading this.

I knew my dad was broken
knew he always put his image first

but I'd never stopped
to consider

that he might have lied
to the police

> *Girls these days
> will say anything . . .*

for I have no doubt
he believed me.

It's only that my story
didn't matter more

than the story he wanted to tell
about himself.

He simply didn't care enough
not only about me

but about the girls Brett would go on to hurt
when these charges were dropped

and he remained in youth ministry
for decades

on the word
of another charismatic
man of the cloth.

I thought this book
was about long-resolved history
but now instead of polishing
the story I thought I knew
like the most oft-repeated scripture

I spend frantic weeks
trying to verify this,
knowing it will be questioned
      a woman's word
      is never enough
knowing my dad will deny it.

I request the case file
and wait

needing to see it
in black and white.

Your request is denied.
A search of our files revealed
NO responsive records
based on the information you provided.

Please note, [we] maintain
a 10-year retention policy
for criminal history and case information
for all
               but the most
                  serious criminal charges.

Your request is now closed.

I shouldn't have hoped.
I knew it was a long shot
when I requested my case file
thirty years after the abuse

but the website said
in sex crimes
and cases involving children
records were held longer
        (but not how much longer).

So I let myself hope
in a country
that reelects a man
who grabs women by the pussy

who tried to stock his cabinet
with four people accused
of sexual assault
of enabling child sexual abuse
and only one was denied

that a lone police department
with an officer actively
advocating for my abuser
might have somehow
cared to preserve
the truths I told them.

This is a truth
I can't see in black and white
a woman's history unpreserved
like so many before mine.

I have to piece
jagged bits together
weigh who I trust
against who I don't.

Tom makes phone calls,
talks to former colleagues.

> *Joy's trying to find out*
> *if someone undermined her*
> *to the police.*

> *You mean her dad?*

Like it's obvious.
This former colleague
has a theory
that Brett had knowledge
of my dad's affairs
and used it as leverage.

I brought my charges up
before my dad's affairs came out
so this horrifying, life-altering idea

        makes twisted sense.

My dad denies it
when I summon the courage
to ask him.

He wasn't being blackmailed.
He didn't tell anyone I was troubled.

He has disparaging things to say
about the specialist in church sexual abuse

and he makes sure to point out
as he has every time we've discussed this

that my sister
                only
                            told him
Brett had kissed her.

He puts the blame on her
for not giving him more details

not making him realize
this was abuse, this was rape

and I wonder where the line was
that would have driven him

to protect me?

How many kisses?
How many fingers?
How many *sluts* and *whores*?

Dear Anna,

Each time I think I've unearthed every horror in my story and fought for my peace with it, some new skeleton pokes a bone out of the endlessly turned earth. Will it ever end?

There's this thing survivors do where they compare their trauma to others' and discount their right to compassion or anger or justice. If it wasn't a stranger with a gun, or they weren't a child, or they weren't utterly alone in the world, do they have any right to their festering wounds?

I've worked hard to avoid this pull, but I find myself falling into it with you. You simply could not catch a break. I cannot fathom how you carried on through the onslaught.

When you found out you were pregnant, it might have been the first stroke of luck in your life—a chance to escape the monotony of service, build a modest life with the father, raising the child you'd made together—except that when you told him of these dreams and the child growing inside you, he fled.

You were not defeated. At least, not for long.

You bore the child and you would find a way to support this tiny family of two, even if it meant cleaning up other people's messes for the rest of your life. The first night you drifted off together you dreamed of what your baby would grow to be and not of how you would be blamed when you woke and found him still and cold.

Babies die. You'd seen it again and again in the houses where you'd served. They're fragile things in a cruel world. Perhaps, you even thought, they're better off.

Well. You thought that until your own child died in the night, here one day and gone the next, and as you grieved the darkest depths of your life, you were dragged to the stocks to be mocked and scorned and blamed.

Those seeking meaning in cruelty weren't satisfied by the steady stream of tears down your face into the mud at your feet. They sentenced you to six years of house arrest for the crime of losing a child.

You weren't defeated. How, I can't understand. But you had the survival instinct to know you couldn't stay in that place, in your sister's home where she judged you too, another mouth to feed, a woman who hadn't been mother enough for the child to stay.

You slipped out into the night and walked until blisters formed and burst and bled but eventually you found yourself on the doorstep of a family who needed a maid. You stayed and caught the eye of Melchior, the landowner's son, too young for you and above your station, besides.

But for whatever reason you intrigued him—did trauma draw him in and then repulse him?—and he listened. It's a low bar when a man who'll listen is all you need to give your heart away (or at least your body, for a time) but so much had been taken from you and at least you could have pleasure.

You couldn't keep the baby that resulted from that pleasure, though. Melchior said he loved you, but it wasn't enough to overcome the fact that he was a wealthy doctor and you a disgraced servant. So even though this baby lived, he was ripped from your arms and you never saw him again.

You were not defeated. *How?*

How do I face the horrifying possibility that my father not only didn't protect me, but may have actively worked against me to protect himself? How do I face the horrifying reality that I may never know the full truth, but I find this version completely plausible, and I cannot trust his? When is it ever going to end?

You left yet another village behind and walked toward an unknown future, believing somehow there was still a reason to put one foot in front of the other. The men you could forget, but you carried your two babies with you, weighing down your steps, etching your footsteps into the Swiss countryside.

When you could not walk another step, you found another employer in another village—no lowly soldier this time, but a physician, a magistrate, a man of power.

At forty-two you were old enough to avoid another child who'd only break your heart. You would have avoided another man if you could have. He'd break your heart too, and he'd know what he was doing.

But when the physician, magistrate, man of power who'd granted you work and room and board decided he wanted to use that power over you, there were two choices: Leave, and walk yet again into the unknown where the next man with power might not have such gentle words, or give him what he wanted and hope—*where did you summon hope?*—it would be enough to secure your place.

You should have left, uncertainty the better choice over a man who wields power as a weapon. But that's so easy for me to say from here. And I know as well as you that gentle words will wear a woman down as sure as rough shoe leather will blister a foot that must keep walking.

Besides, you cared for him, believed there was finally one good man. Not good enough, though, to keep you employed when his wife began to suspect his indiscretions.

You didn't ask the impossible. After Melchior, you'd never dream to rise above your station, but you wouldn't be discarded again. If he didn't want you to reveal his secrets, he would have to let you keep your position. You would not be defeated.

At least until he called you a witch.

A witch hadn't burned in those parts for thirty years. This was the Enlightenment, the age of reason, science, logic. Women did not consort with the devil, eating babies at the Sabbath, kissing the devil's ass, and causing children to vomit pins.

Unless you were a man of power who felt the world's structures shifting beneath your very feet and an inconvenient woman would not be defeated.

You didn't burn. That would have been cruel. Instead, your head was parted from your body by a sword, the only thing that could stop your forward march.

Finally you rested.

For two hundred years, and then your name was upon the lips of men of power again. This time Swiss legislators pardoned you, though the Protestant church stood against the decision. Apparently it takes more than two hundred years for some to take responsibility.

I'm so glad you weren't around for that last indignity, Anna. You went through enough.

Anna Göldi
(1734–1782, Switzerland)
Anna was a household servant placed under house arrest when her baby died. She escaped to have another baby with someone above her station; it was taken from her. Another employer accused her of witchcraft when she threatened to tell his wife of their sexual involvement.

I'm so tired.
The endless cycle:
contacting a church
where Brett has moved,
sending that first email,
waiting for the response,
having the conversations
	(if they respond at all)
and then being dismissed again.

Then the nagging feeling
in the back of my head,
a low-key buzz, tinnitus of trauma,
constant in the background
as I chase toddlers
and pass endless nights
reassuring them of their safety.

> He's unchecked, in charge
> of a group of young people,
> molding them, shaping them,
> free to target any girl
> who's the right kind of vulnerable
> all because I didn't
> stay in that car that night
> and tell Logan to drive.

> The years of therapy
> will teach me
> this isn't my burden,
> but it doesn't stop
> the endless litany.

> Funny how I never

        entertain the thought
        that I might have avoided
        the abuse entirely;
        only that I might have
        stopped him sooner
        when proof (beyond my word)
        might have been within reach.

I wait until the buzzing is too much to bear
and I fall down an internet rabbit hole again,
searching for his latest church
and it all begins anew.

As I write this
I realize I should check
if he's still at the church
he's been at for ages.

He's not.
I don't let myself hope
this means he's been stopped.
I simply begin the grim exercise
of scouring the internet.

I find him
still in ministry
and back in the San Diego suburbs.

I text my friend Krista.
She was with me
in the youth group
and over the decades
we've only grown closer.

He's back.

I'm stunned
but numb to the idea
of taking any action.

Krista's response
is visceral and immediate.
She still lives in the area,
could run into him
on the street
and worse than that
is a mother of teens.

The audacity
to return to the area
where many of our friends from youth group
are now the parents of teens.

Krista calls
the current senior pastor
of the church we grew up in.
He knows this history
and is willing to help.

        What can I do?

                I need someone to contact the church
                and tell them he's a predator.

Okay. That's what I'll do.

This pastor reaches out
to Brett's current employers.

We gather
over Zoom, making this
the first time I'll speak
(virtually) face-to-face
with one of his churches.
      Vivid memory
      of speaking on the phone
      to a pastor who asked
           Why didn't you speak up sooner?
      with my son strapped to my chest
      in a baby carrier.

On the call:

Krista, whose face I focus on

Tom, ever steady

Sheila, my mom's best friend
      who had kids in Brett's youth group
      and became a pastor
      after I left the church

Joe, my junior high youth pastor
      who left that church
      because of Brett
      and is now a senior pastor
      in another San Diego suburb

the current senior pastor
      of the church I grew up in
      who is lovely and supportive
      and I still panic when I receive an email
      because his name is also Brett

and the senior pastor
executive pastor
and human resources director
of my abuser's current church.

They are baffled to learn
Brett has history in the area.
His ministry résumé begins
in 2006, they tell us.

But he began his ministry
in 1992.

Which means
there are fourteen years
he doesn't want anyone
asking about.

We learn they serve
a large population
of military families

providing an array
of young women
whose fathers
or husbands
are away
for long stretches of time.

Ideal hunting grounds
for a hungry predator
in the guise of
comforting father figure
to have his fill.

      Hypothetically, of course, Your Honor.

I tell my story
out loud
directly to people
who work with him daily,
watch their faces
as I spare no detail.

   I believe you,
    the senior pastor says.

Four months later
Brett is still pictured
on their website under
      Our Leaders.

Tom reaches out
so I don't have to correspond directly
with the people I already know
in my gut
have chosen to ignore
my history.

Our investigation is complete
and all the information
was presented to our Leadership Board.

We've worked with Brett
for almost three years
and we have seen no evidence
of sexual inappropriateness.

The Leadership Board prayerfully decided
to retain Brett
because the police would not press charges
and no one has made allegations of misconduct
at the multiple churches
Brett has worked at
over the past 30 years.

While this may not be the outcome
you have hoped for
we ask that you respect our process
and treat us with love
as fellow Christ followers.

Sincerely,

Pastor of Discipleship and Young Families

Immediately after
I read this email
I have to go with my daughter
to the theater where we both work.

I'm shaking.
I ask her to drive.
She knows the broad strokes
of what's been happening
so I tell her the final nail
in the coffin of my hope
that this monster
will ever be stopped.

My daughter, nineteen,
usually deeply eloquent,
is plain.

That fucking sucks.

We arrive at the theater
for opening night
of the new play festival
and I plaster on a smile

do my best
to greet colleagues
who believe with their whole hearts
that telling stories makes a difference in the world

        tonight's play
        about two queer kids
        helping each other survive
        oppressive religion and abusive parents

while knowing
that I have told this story
again and again and again
obliquely, directly
in writing, out loud
for decades on decades
and nothing ever changes.

Blood Water Paint
came out in 2018
only months after the #MeToo
resurgence on Twitter
and over and over I heard,

> *It's so timely.*

It's still timely
seven years later
as sex offenders run the country

and it was timely in 2015
when *Blood Water Paint* premiered as a play

and it was timely in 2001
when I first learned of Artemisia Gentileschi

and it was timely in 1998
when I brought the charges forward

and it was timely in 1993, 1994, 1995
when I was being abused

and it was timely in 1991
when Anita Hill was demeaned and dismissed
as she testified during the confirmation hearings
of future Supreme Court Justice Clarence Thomas
about years of sexual harassment

and it was timely in 1984,
the very beginning of a Biblical flood
of allegations within the Catholic Church,
when Father Gilbert Gauthe

was finally convicted
after abusing thirty-seven children,
served only ten years and emerged
from prison to abuse a three-year-old

and it was timely in 1982
when, according to Dr. Christine Blasey Ford's
testimony to congress,
future Supreme Court Justice Brett Kavanaugh
assaulted her at a high school party

and it was timely in 1974
when Congress passed
the Child Abuse Prevention and Treatment Act,
establishing mandatory reporting laws

and it was timely in 1972
when women at the University of South Florida
donned black capes and brooms
and marched through campus,
Taking Back the Night

and it was timely in 1969
when Bill Cosby, whose show my family
watched together every Thursday night.
started joking about drugging women
so he could have sex with them

and it was timely in 1612
when Artemisia's hands were crushed
in a courtroom to verify her story
while her rapist watched

and it was timely in the first century
when Judith sliced off Holofernes's head
because no one else would do
a goddamn thing
to protect the vulnerable.

Triggers

tongue in my ear
hand on my head

    my son
    goes through a toddler phase
    of patting me on the head
    which should be adorable
    and instead causes panic

navy blue trucks
boxers

    dogs he got
    after contact ended
    but I was still in his periphery
    so even though I love dogs abundantly
    boxers terrify me

every song
from Brett's mixtapes

    "Oh l'amour"...

church service
praise music
purity culture

a specific mouthwash

    my husband must discard
    multiple bottles
    that come too close

Chili's
wrestling
high school football

dental work

        holding my mouth open
        objects shoved inside
        I learn to request the calming weight
        of the X-ray blanket
        for even the most basic cleaning

palm trees
salt air

Lomas Santa Fe
Via de la Valle
Del Mar Heights

anyone
behind
me

any
unexpected
sound

        my own children
        if I don't know they're there

I startle
at the mildest surprise,
my body frozen
in fight or flight,
always prepared for extreme peril.

If someone speaks behind me
rounds a corner
appears in a doorway

I startle
except that word is too mild
for the sudden panic
that jolts through my body.
I scream in terror
at the sight
of my beloveds

and I hate myself
every time
and then I hate myself
for hating myself
because my body
is only trying
to protect me.

Often I cry.
My family learns
to tap walls
and flip lights
on their approach.
We hang bells
in the kitchen doorway
since I must stand

with my back to it
when I'm cooking.

You've been running from a bear
for twenty years, a doctor says
when I finally seek help,
when I finally understand
that even if the root is trauma
the result is physiological.

This is before
the women of the internet declare
that we would run toward a bear
rather than a man in the woods.

The doctor might have said,
You've been running from Brett
for twenty years.

She gives me medications
that help the panic attacks
the incessant nightmares

but nothing lessens
the fight or flight.

Complex PTSD
involves repetitive, prolonged trauma
with direct harm, exploitation, and maltreatment
including neglect

by ostensibly responsible adults
which occurs at
        developmentally vulnerable times
in a survivor's life.

                      I am fifteen.
                      I am sixteen.
                      I am seventeen.

Traumatic stressors are
events, experiences, and exposures

                      betrayal
                      slut
                      whore

that greatly exceed
the individual's capacity
to control, cope with, or withstand
and cause fundamental and life-altering
psychophysiological harm.

                      It's a need for tangible pain.

Other types of complex trauma:

relational or interpersonal,
in which an individual is trapped
for an extended period of time

in an abusive relationship with someone
in a position of authority over them.

> You have to stay.
> You're here as a leader.

institutional,
in which ongoing trauma
is inflicted by the actions
or lack of actions
on the part of an institution

like a church

> Girls these days
> will say anything.

or justice system.

> She claims her father
> let her read my case file—

> inconsistent, full of lies.

With thanks to Dr. Christine A. Courtois
and Dr. Julian D. Ford, eds, in their 2020 book,
*Treating Complex Traumatic Stress Disorders in Adults:
Scientific Foundations and Therapeutic Models*

Neglected kids
have holes in their shoes
threadbare clothes
teeth decaying from malnutrition.

I had a middle-class roof over my head
two parents with college degrees
who paid for a math tutor
and voice lessons
and orthodontia.

There was always
enough food
if only
I would eat it.

But also
even after
my sister told my father
who this youth pastor was

no one ever questioned
the late nights
the excessive time
I spent alone with him,
the control he had
over my life.

                                      They had him over
                                      for Thanksgiving.

My dad visits me in Seattle
and while his wife
takes my kids out for ice cream
he confronts me
over comments I've posted
on Twitter about him

typical snark
from an adult child
about a frustrating parent
on a platform
the parent doesn't
       to her knowledge
frequent.

Except he does,
searching for my name,
reading my posts.

       For book news.

Nearly every comment
he objects to
comes back to my hurt
that he doesn't listen.

He wants to litigate
each specific slight.
I see no point
when the original wound
is still gaping.

The only thing
I need from you
is an apology
with no excuses
or justifications.

I have my husband
at my side
for this conversation
because I know what's coming,
because I'll need another rational person
to tell me later
that I heard what I thought I heard.

The exact opposite
of what I asked for.

> *You have to understand*
> *your sister didn't tell me everything . . .*
>
> *It wasn't only me;*
> *I consulted the youth elder . . .*

I suppose I should have seen
what nobody else did . . .

Exasperated excuses
deflections, justifications.
Making me the fool
for placing any blame on him.

Leading to:

You can't play the abuse card forever.

I go to the kitchen
to make more tea,
needing a break
from the dizzying circles

but he follows me
and when I turn around
to see him, startled,
and scream

                    my brain, my body
                    in constant readiness
                    for assault

he huffs
and rolls his eyes
at my overreaction.

I've always been so dramatic.

Dear Joan,

I learned your story—or at least some man's version—by pulling another play off my father's bookshelf and reading *Saint Joan* by George Bernard Shaw, who believed your accusers had been mistreated by history.

Poor babies.

But he showed me enough of your story to leave me awestruck. How did an illiterate peasant girl with no military training convince the crown prince to give her an army? I suppose it doesn't matter. It happened, indisputable facts in the historical record. Of the countless women who donned men's clothes and fought in wars, yours is one of the few names we know with any certainty.

Still, I can't help but marvel at your confidence, your conviction, your faith in yourself and your God.

After all that—fighting to be heard, proving yourself to the crown prince, leading an army to victory at Orléans—what a shock when you were captured, that what they were most concerned with was your trousers.

What did she wear? Again and again. Breezy romper for the desert heat or long trousers appropriate for battle—either way we both refused to understand our place.

In their judgment against you, they called you *a pernicious temptress, presumptuous, credulous, rash, superstitious, a false prophetess, a blasphemer against God and his saints, scornful of God in his sacraments, a transgressor of divine law, sacred doctrine and ecclesiastical decrees, seditious, cruel, apostate, and schismatic.*

I mean, same.

You may be the most famous person ever burned at the stake on charges of witchcraft who no one truly believed was a witch. You were something far more terrifying:

a girl who didn't need a man to speak to God in order to hear him and follow his commands.

a girl who stood your ground, so devoted to chastity that you took your father to court to avoid marriage.

a girl who time and again wanted nothing of what the world wanted for you.

You could have lost your faith in a god who would use you, then abandon you, a helpless girl in chains, to the mercy of prison guards. Perhaps you did, in moments. But perhaps, like me, you couldn't shake the belief that he was still out there, he was still good, he still loved you despite the irreparable brokenness of his people.
But did you also wonder sometimes if that made you a fool?
I don't need to tell your story. It's one of the few of its kind most people know. But you have helped me tell mine, Joan.

To the girl who can't sit still
on the hard-backed pews
while the preacher teaches
from dusty tomes divined by men for men:

Their God squeezes everything
to dust in an unforgiving fist
because that's the only way
they understand power.

What if God wants
you to wiggle off that pew
and dance out into the world
to spread her love with open arms?

Joan of Arc
(c 1412–1431, France)
Joan was an illiterate peasant who heard voices from God and led the French to victory over the English. When she was captured, the English brought seventy charges against her, many related to her short hair and men's clothing, as well as witchcraft. Joan confessed in exchange for life imprisonment, but when she went back to wearing men's clothing and hearing voices, she was executed as a "relapsed heretic."

Maybe
like that French peasant girl
I too can talk to God
in my own way.

Maybe the church and I
are both too broken
and some pieces
have gone missing
along the way
so we will never
be made whole.

It doesn't mean
I don't believe
the things I preached
from the pulpit
all those years ago:

> *In the beginning was the Word*
> *and the Word was with God*
> *and the Word was God*

but I can never listen to that Word
from a man in a pulpit again.

A gifted young writer
sees me talking on Twitter
about my abuse

posting on the hashtag
#churchtoo

about being assaulted
by my youth pastor

and is astonished
to realize
she is not the only one.

She reads *Blood Water Paint*
and signs up for an online class
I'm teaching on verse novels.

The first time she shares
I'm mesmerized
by her voice, her courage.
She writes her own verse novel

telling her story
on the page
and in a courtroom
sending her rapist to prison
and refusing to be silenced.

Telling my story has changed a life.

PART III

The next time
I'm gripped
with unrelenting pains
blamed on Eve's
pursuit of knowledge

I'm doing it my way.

I've found a midwife
who'll allow my pregnancy to go late,
understanding I've inherited knowledge
about my own body
from the women who came before me.

I creep from the bedroom,
trying not to wake
my four-year-old daughter
though she'll emerge soon
to the sound of my husband
inflating the birth pool
and calling the midwife.

My doula is at another birth
but sends a replacement
I've never met
but whose peacock tattoo
is burned into my mind
more than a decade later.

My midwife arrives
with two assistants;
my aunt comes next
to tend to my daughter.

The house fills with women
who'll get me through this.

Foremothers

Eve,
you labored
with no understanding
of what was happening to your body;

Eufame,
you suffered
and wished
as we all do
for relief;

Anna,
you labored in birth
but never got the reward
of motherhood;

Katherine,
you tried to provide
for your daughters
from your first moment till the last;

Bridget,
you were no stranger to pain
when you delivered children
into a home where
they would always know violence;

Sarah,
mother of little Dorothy,
you lost one baby in prison,
knowing your small child
was also being held
through no fault of hers
        (or yours).

If you could do this,
I will survive it, too.

I want this birth
to be a beautiful healing,
taking back control,
my body in its power.

It's not.
It's brutal,
relentless.

There are no breaks
between contractions.
The midwife tells me
not to yell so loud,
to save my energy,
but I will not
be silenced again.

She tells me to get out of the water,
it's too cold for my body to relax
but it's the only place I feel close to safe,
so I stay, shivering, moaning,
sure I'm going to die.

When the baby finally comes,
there's no beatific photo
of me cradling him in the water.
I look agonized, as though
I've been through
thumbscrews and thrawing.

Even after the baby's out
it's not over. Hands are reaching,
pulling, tugging. The placenta
must also release, but it resists.
With no warning, the midwife
twists my nipple.

Finally the placenta comes
and I'm on my own bed
with my baby snuggled beside me
but the contractions continue,
the uterus shrinking back to size.

Last time, in the wake
of my daughter's C-section
lingering anesthesia dulled these pains
but now I feel every spasm

and I don't blame Eve
but I do think it's a pretty shitty trick
that half the world bears this weight
with everything else
already upon our shoulders.

Instead of abuse
my husband found welcome
in a Presbyterian church
as a boy whose mother
had died too soon.

We met in this church
in Guatemala
where I was startled
to realize

        how similar
        the services were to the ones
        I'd grown up with

the language and liturgy
only translated into Spanish
even the same logo on the bulletins

and there's a tiny redemption
in this iglesia presbiteriana
finally leading me to
a man I can trust.

After we married
and settled in Seattle
he patiently followed me
as I searched for a church
that didn't send my heart
careening in panic.

It never happened.

My daughter reaches high school
and attends the youth group
of my husband's church.

>I go sometimes
>but more often than not
>Sunday mornings find me
>physically ill, my body telling me
>what my mind doesn't know how to.

I talk to her about purity culture,
give her all the tools I wish I'd had.
She rolls her eyes. She knows these things.
She's so solid, steady in who she is,
the language of feminism and social justice
as natural to her as English and Spanish.

But will it be enough
if someone comes along
and sees her lying on the ground
after Bible study, singing with her friends?
A newlywed young youth pastor
sends all my alarm bells ringing
based on nothing but history

but that feels justified
after millennia of women
have been convicted
based on nothing
but their existence.

She reaches a gap year
before college
her younger brother
just entering high school.

She knows my story.
He understands why
she gets pepper spray
in her Christmas stocking.

Together we talk to him
about how to use his privilege
how to be an ally
why women choose the bear.

Why, as he grows
into a male athlete's body
he might make a woman nervous
on the street or public transit
and that's not a judgment on him
but on a world that's given her
every reason to fear him.

They are my heart
beating outside my body
in a world
I know to be both
cruel and beautiful

but I have done everything I can
to prepare them
and if they should face trauma

        and I know they might

they will face it
with my support
my fury

my blade forged
in this unrelenting inferno.

I mash lemon balm leaves
with coconut oil
in a mortar and pestle
and apply the paste
to my daughter's bug bites.
It relieves the irritation
and with a grin
she calls me a witch.

I brew a tea
from chamomile and lemon balm
I've grown in my garden
to relieve my daughter's cramps
       (oh Eve, I promise
         we don't blame you)
and again she calls me
that affectionate name:
            witch.

She draws
      oh, she constantly creates
a study on witches
that I keep above my desk,
four women in pen and ink:

      a child trying on a pointy hat
      a young woman working plant magic
      an old crone bewitching animals
      a grave sorceress bending light.

I want to be
the witch she sees in me.

I'm a book witch
kitchen witch
garden witch

cozy witch
stitching curses
crafting verses
spinning a world
safe for me and mine

never forgetting
the weight
of that word

the women lost
because the world
feared their power.

I'm crazy
unstable, a liar.

You can tell yourself that
if it makes you feel safe,
you patriarchs, cowering
behind collars and robes

craven serpents rattling power
like it will distract history
from your ghastly deeds.

You're not safe.

You're propped up
on a pedestal
built by your fellows
with nothing
but your own fear
for fuel.

What if your foundation cracks
what if the lies
it's all built upon
                      shift

what if the slightest wind comes along
and everything you convinced yourself
                            convinced the world was true
crumbles to dust?

You want a witch?
Here I am,
always with a dog
familiar at my side.

Old crone hair
that whitened
when my body
was still young.

I brew potions
and anger neighbors.
I'm a loudmouthed woman
teaching my children
to demand their autonomy

while constantly reminding myself
that I've got it now, I'm safe.

But you're not.

I'm a tempest
howling truth
like the weapon it is,
even as you bind me
to the stake.

You can't shut me up.
Go on, build your little fire
beneath my feet.
You think there's enough
smoke in the world
to choke down this voice
I honed against your steel,
to silence my warnings
my invocation
to the ones who follow?

Because it doesn't end with me.
That's a lie
flimsier
than this scaffolding.

Your kindling catches fire
and I feel the heat
licking at my skin
but joke's on you—
witch-marks
already cover my body,
the record of my survival
etched into my skin
telling my story
from the moment Eve bit that apple
to the moment you try to burn me down

and I summon all the stories
of the survivors before me
and together we unite our power,
casting a spell that turns
your feeble fire against you

                and once you've burnt
                we grind your ashes to dust
                beneath our dance.

A NOTE ON THE COVER PAINTING

"Jael and Sisera" is a 1620 painting by Artemisia Gentileschi, depicting a scene from the Book of Judges, in which Jael, a woman of the nomadic Kenite tribe drives a tent stake through the head of Sisera, a brutal Canaanite commander. It's a story I never learned growing up in the church, and though Biblical stories were common subjects for the painters of Artemisia's day, few depicted this one.

It's an uncomfortable story. If a male soldier had struck down Sisera with a sword, Biblical scholars would classify him as an Israelite hero. But when a woman used her domestic tools—as a nomadic woman, setting up and striking the tents was in her purview—to bring down a vicious enemy to Israel, suddenly commentators are torn on how to interpret her.

Artemisia wasn't torn. She depicts a Jael who is calm and thoughtful, emotionally composed, and ready for the gruesome task at hand. She depicts not the bloody gore of her more famous work, Judith Slaying Holofernes, but the moment of resolve, right before justice is enacted. Artemisia understood Jael as a woman in a world dominated by men who used the humble tools at hand to leave her mark on history.

ACKNOWLEDGMENTS

Writing a memoir is a process of unearthing huge traumas and trying to make sense of the rubble once the earth has stopped shaking. As I worked on this book, unimaginable aftershocks made me doubt the upheaval would ever stop. I couldn't have written this without the steadying hands of the following people, who made sure I didn't fall (or helped me up when I did).

To my mother and sister, I know my story intersects with your own stories, and that you have your versions of this time. I am so grateful to you for your blessing to tell my own story in my own way.

I am enormously indebted to a number of friends from high school who shared their memories of this time. To Laurel Messer, Cara Miller, Paula Taylor, thank you for your steadfast belief in and support of me. To Jarrod, Trevor, and Brian, thank you for being good guys from the start. Thank you all for reflecting on a difficult time as I wrote this book. I am grateful beyond measure—memory and trauma are tricky, and your recollections helped so much.

Special thanks to Heather Caliri, who has been with me and this manuscript every step of the way, reading an early draft, answering my random and sometimes disturbing texts as I revised, and generally being a wonderful friend and fellow writer in the trenches of memoir and trauma. I'm so glad to have had your friendship in high school, but even more so to have it now as adults.

And also to Jim Hancock, who is called Tom in the book. If his name is familiar, it may be because my previous novel, *Everything Is Poison*, was dedicated to Jim and his wife, Susan, in gratitude for giving me a safe place to turn. This book tells the story behind that dedication. Jim, you were a rock through the events of this book, and your careful recordkeeping from the days of a college email address I no longer have access to was invaluable during both the writing and the legal review. I'm so glad we're neighbors now.

Enormous thanks go to my agent, Jim McCarthy, who didn't even blink when I said I'd written a thing that was kind of a memoir but also kind of about historical witch trials. Your support, flexibility, and faith in me is a gift I couldn't have fathomed when I set out on my publishing journey. Thank you also to everyone at Dystel, Goderich, and Bourret for supporting Jim in supporting my work.

I do not have sufficient words to thank my editor, Andrew Karre, for the care with which you handle every book, but especially this one. Your thoughtful questions and insight, your outrage and your fury, did more for me than many years of therapy. (Although thank you to all the therapists, too!) Thank you for allowing me to make you a character in this book. It was inevitable from the moment you said, "I think this should be a writer's memoir." Truly, I am so astonished by the honor of working with you.

Theresa Evangelista and Anna Booth, you always make my books beautiful through artistic witchcraft I cannot comprehend but absolutely appreciate. Thank you for a cover I couldn't have begun to dream up but fits so perfectly. (And to Artemisia, for the original art, of course.)

Thank you to Julie Strauss-Gabel, Rob Farren, Natalie Melius, Rye White, Madison Penico, Ilana Jacobs, [COPYEDITOR], and [PROOFREADER], for your advocacy and attention to detail. Thank you to Jordana Kulak and everyone in marketing, sales, and publicity whose names I never even hear but I know you are doing incredible work. Special thanks to the School & Library crew—Carmela Iaria, Venessa Carson, Summer Ogata, Trevor Ingerson, Judith Huerta, Danielle Presley, and Gaby Paez for your tireless work getting my books into the hands of teachers and librarians.

Thank you to author friends Stephanie Kuehnert, for support in the process of writing and publishing memoir, and Erin Hahn, for early feedback on the manuscript. Thank you to Maggie Lee and Todd Matthews for helping me track down some elusive figures. Thank you to Bob and Suzie

Rantzow for additional records and recollections, and for introducing me to the healing power of dogs. Barney and Nina helped me survive this time.

And thank you, of course, most of all and always, to my husband and two wonderful children for your patient and gentle love. I am blessed beyond measure to share my life with you. I might startle every time you come around a corner, but I never doubt for one second that I am safe with you.

NOTES

ON NAMES

Other than my name and the names of public or historical figures, all names in this book have been changed.

More TK

SELECTED BIBLIOGRAPHY

Barstow, Anne Llewellyn. *Joan of Arc: Heretic, Mystic, Shaman* (Lewiston: E. Mellen Press, 1986).

Barstow. "On Studying Witchcraft as Women's History: A Historiography of the European Witch Persecutions," *Journal of Feminist Studies in Religion*, vol. 4, no. 2 (Fall 1988), pp. 7–19.

Barstow. *Witchcraze: A New History of the European Witch Hunts* (New York: HarperCollins, 1994).

Ben-Yehuda, Nachman. "The European Witch Craze of the 14th to 17th Centuries: A Sociologist's Perspective," *American Journal of Sociology*, vol. 86, no. 1 (July 1980), pp. 1–31.

Christ-Doane, Rachel. "The Untold Story of Dorothy Good, Salem's Youngest Accused Witch," https://salemwitchmuseum.com/wp-content/uploads/2024/01/The-Untold-Story-of-Dorothy-Good.pdf.

Detweiler, Robert. "Shifting Perspectives on the Salem Witches," *The History Teacher*, vol. 8, no. 4 (August 1975), pp. 596–610.

Foulds, Diane E. *Death in Salem: The Private Lives Behind the 1692 Witch Hunt* (City TK: Globe Pequot PR, 2010).

Goodare, Julian. "The Framework for Scottish Witch-Hunting in the 1590s," *The Scottish Historical Review*, vol. 81, no. 212, part 2 (October 2002), pp. 240-50.

Goss, K. David. *Daily Life During the Salem Witch Trials* (City TK: Greenwood, 2012).

Heaton, Claude Edwin. "The History of Anesthesia and Analgesia in Obstetrics," *Journal of the History of Medicine and Allied Sciences*, vol. 1, no. 4, Anesthesia Centennial Number (October 1946), pp. 567-72.

Lagerlöf-Génetay, Birgitta. *The Beginning of the Swedish Witch Trials 1668-1671* (Stockholm: Akademitryck AB, 1990).

Levack, Brian P. *The Witch Hunt in Early Modern Europe*, fourth ed. (Abingdon, UK: Routledge, 2016).

MacBain, Jenny. *The Salem Witch Trials: A Primary Source History of the Witchcraft Trials in Salem, Massachusetts* (New York: Rosen Central, 2003).

Roach, Marilynne K. The Salem Witch Trials: A Day-by-Day Chronicle of a Community Under Siege (City TK: Cooper Square Press, 2002).

Roach. *Six Women of Salem: The Untold Story of the Accused and Their Accusers in the Salem Witch Trials* (Boston: Da Capo Press, 2013).

Schiff, Stacy. *The Witches: Salem, 1692* (New York: Little, Brown, 2015).

Spoto, Stephanie Irene. "Jacobean Witchcraft and Feminine Power,"*Pacific Coast Philology*, vol. 45 (2010), pp. 53-70.

Wasser, Michael. "The Privy Council and the Witches: The Curtailment of Witchcraft Prosecutions in Scotland, 1597-1628," *The Scottish Historical Review*, vol. 82, no. 213, part 1 (April 2003), pp. 20-46.

Yeoman, Louise. "The woman who stood up to a witch-hunt," BBC Scotland, November 9, 2019.

"Anna Goeldi's story and exoneration". BBC News, September 20, 2007.

NOTES

000 Dear Eufame: Claude Edwin Heaton, "The History of Anesthesia and Analgesia in Obstetrics,", *Journal of the History of Medicine and Allied Sciences*, vol. 1, no. 4, Anesthesia Centennial Number (October 1946), pp. 567–572.

000 Dear Dorothy: https://salemwitchmuseum.com/wp-content/uploads/2024/01/The-Untold-Story-of-Dorothy-Good.pdf.

000 Dear Abigail: Diane E. Foulds, *Death in Salem: The Private Lives Behind the 1692 Witch Hunt*, Globe Pequot PR, 2010.

000 Dear Elizabeth: Marilynne K. Roach, *The Salem Witch Trials: A Day-by-Day Chronicle of a Community Under Siege*, Cooper Square Press, 2002.

000 Dear Salem Girls: Foulds, Death in Salem.

000 Dear Ann: Roach, *Six Women of Salem: The Untold Story of the Accused and Their Accusers in the Salem Witch Trials*, Da Capo Press, 2013.

000 Dear Gertrud: Birgitta Lagerlöf-Génetay, *The Beginning of the Swedish Witch Trials 1668–1671*, Akademitryck AB, 1990.

000 Dear Geillis: Julian Goodare, "The Framework for Scottish Witch-Hunting in the 1590s," *The Scottish Historical Review*, vol. 81, no. 212, part 2 (October 2002), pp. 240–50.

000 I've thought about that law student: www.bonjeanlaw.com/jenniferbonjean (retrieved June 30, 2025).

000 "I'm supposed to be some type of": www.nytimes.com/2022/09/19/arts/music/jennifer-bonjean-r-kelly-bill-cosby.html (retrieved June 30, 2025).

000 Dear Marion: Louise Yeoman, "The woman who stood up to a witch-hunt," BBC Scotland, November 9, 2019.

000 it took her so long to come forward: https://www.nytimes.com/2022/09/19/arts/music/jennifer-bonjean-r-kelly-bill-cosby.html (retrieved June 30, 2025).

000 "Boy, did Judy and Donna enjoy themselves": www.nytimes.com/live/2022/06/21/arts/bill-cosby-verdict-judy-huth#judy-huth-playboy-mansion (retrieved June 30, 2025).

000 According to California Penal Code: Penal Code § 11165.7, https://leginfo.legislature.ca.gov/faces/codes_displaySection.xhtml?sectionNum=11165.7&lawCode=PEN (retrieved June 30, 2025).

000 Dear Christian: Brian P. Levack, *The Witch Hunt in Early Modern Europe*, fourth ed., Routledge, 2016.

000 "I remember this case very well": TKTKTK.

000 Dear Katherine: Anne Llewellyn Barstow, *Witchcraze: A New History of the European Witch Hunts*, HarperCollins, 1994.

000 Dear Bridget: Roach, Six Women of Salem.

000 "the most painful was Paul's decision": TKTKTKTK.

000 "Your request is denied": TKTKTKTK.

000 Dear Anna: "Anna Goeldi's story and exoneration," [as in bibliography, please confirm au name and article title for this] BBC News. September 20, 2007.

000 "Our investigation is complete": TKTKTK.

000 *Treating Complex Traumatic Stress Disorders in Adults: Scientific Foundations and Therapeutic Models*: TKTKTK.

000 Dear Joan: Barstow, *Joan of Arc: Heretic, Mystic, Shaman*, E. Mellen, 1986.

A NOTE ABOUT THE TYPE

Edita is a font family designed by Pilar Cano and released in 2010. Cano intended Edita to be "humanist in concept yet with a contemporary feel where softness and fluidity play a very important role."